HOW TO TAKE
IMMEDIATE CONTROL
Of Your
MIND & LIFE

NARESH KUMAR

Naresh Kumar
Flat-105, Vars Notting Hill, 1st Main, TC Palya Main Road, Ramamurthy Nagar, Bangalore 560016
Published in Bangalore, India

Printed and Bound by Pothi.com
Mudranik Technologies Pvt Ltd
#634, Ground Floor,
5th Main, Indiranagar 2nd Stage,
Bangalore 560038

First Printing 2019
First Edition 2019

10 9 8 7 6 5 4 3 2 1

Legal Disclaimer

"One can have no greater mastery than mastery of oneself."

~ Leonardo Da Vinci

Table of Contents

CHAPTER 1
INTRODUCTION

My journey in personal development started in 1999, when I felt a dire need to work on my own shortcomings. Over the years I did a lot of work towards my personal development and noticed several visible changes in myself. The changes happened, but usually took their own time. Often, I had to continue reading self-help books or keep attending seminars, to sustain my personal development. Whenever I stopped reading – the motivation died within a few days.

In 2014, I bumped into Neuro-Linguistic Programming (NLP). I was surprised at the claims made by various NLPers and to be honest, I was very skeptical. I had previously burned my fingers while pursuing some courses. Anyway, I took a leap of faith after careful considerations – and have never looked back since.

The NLP techniques, are not just quick and effective but the results are also long lasting. For example, if you want to get up early – all that you need is a technique aptly called - New Behavior Generator, once or twice. Each iteration takes just a couple of minutes and then you're set for the rest of your life. Now, not all techniques will be over so fast. Some techniques are pretty complicated and take more time. Also, if you're a helping professional, you may have to do multiple techniques to help the client in complex scenarios. However, the time taken in all cases will usually be a fraction of time than the conventional approaches to achieve the same result.

So, I was stunned by the effectiveness of NLP. It's a tool which worked really fast and was successful for almost 100% of times. To me, I had accidentally bumped into the gold mine of personal development. And I set on a long journey to learn NLP. I did it from multiple sources – books, courses, online resources etc., and upped my credentials. During my first Master Practitioner as attendee, I successfully did two therapies and earned respect of other fellow participants. I also started using NLP in my Coaching. The two successful therapies made me interested in learning Hypnotherapy, EFT and other healing modalities. Apart from this, I continued to work in IT industry and NLP helped me in achieving a peak performance in IT career as well. NLP also helped me in becoming a better father, a better husband and a better person to relate to. In summary, NLP changed my whole life. The only regret, I had after learning NLP was – "Why didn't I learn it five or ten years ago?"

Today, I hold NLP workshop and trainings in India. I also do one-on-one Coaching and Therapy sessions. Thanks to NLP, most of my clients have got far better results than they hoped for, and in some cases even leading to life transforming experiences. I hope to touch many more lives through my workshops, sessions and books, like this one in your hand.

ABOUT THIS BOOK

This book is a collection of techniques which I have used on myself and my clients. I believe anyone can use these techniques and master their mind. Personal Mastery is a process. You will never be able to say you have absolutely mastered yourself – for there are levels after each level. And with each level you gain more control over your mental, emotional, physical and financial destiny.

I would like to encourage you to further explore in the field of NLP, and to use these powerful ideas responsibly with respect and integrity, to create more choices and happiness in your and others lives.

Though this book can serve as a great introductory resource to NLP or as a reference material, it is not a substitute to formal NLP training. NLP is best experienced live. Read the menu, and if you like what you read, enjoy the meal.

So now, let us begin our learning journey and start with an introduction to NLP.

WHAT IS NLP?

NLP is an abbreviation for Neuro-Linguistic Programming. This can be broken down as below:

Neuro: Refers to your neurology. The way you are wired.

Linguistic: The language that you use to communicate with yourself (self-talk) and others. This also includes your body language.

Programming: Refers to your mental programs, i.e., your mental strategies.

You can say that NLP techniques work with the brain (**neuro**) using language (**linguistic**) to program behaviors (**programming**).

Here is another correlation. These three things, i.e. Neurology, Linguistic and Programming, affect each other. For example, take the case when something triggers your angry response – let's say someone's face. And just seeing his face may make you cranky and you may start getting upset at small things. You may start responding harshly to people or start cursing yourself for being stuck with that person.

Hence, you can say that:

the programming (automatic response on seeing person's face) affects

your neurology (feeling cranky, getting upset) and

language (responding harshly).

Now consider, that when all that happens, you become aware of your behavior and you remember your most respected teacher saying – "Everyone has their own map of the world. People respond to their map of the world. And the real way to make someone understand is to look at the situation from their perspective". And due to this internal linguistic chatter you may start calming down. You may start feeling overall relaxed – even your body feels more relaxed and when the next colleague calls you for help – you respond calmly. If this happens a couple of times, the brain generalizes and you stop getting upset at people and always respond calmly.

In short:

the linguistics (internal talk) affects

neurology (calm, relaxed) and

programming (new auto-response to colleague).

Neurology also affects the other two components. For example, as you're reading it, think about some fun activity that you enjoy. Keep thinking about it till you start getting the fun feeling and try to have a negative self-talk at the same time. Try as hard you can. You'll notice that it's not possible to have a positive emotion and negative self-talk together. If you do it few times intentionally, your general mood will shift to more positive and upbeat. Even in tough situations, you will manage to be much happier than others.

Hence,

the neurology (fun state) affects

language (self-talk) and

programming (shift to more positive and upbeat general mood, happiness in the face of problems).

There is no official definition of NLP – except that it's the art of modeling excellence. However, that definition no longer covers all aspects of NLP. Different authors have tried to define it in different ways. Here are some popular definitions of NLP:

- The art and science of excellence

- The art and science of communication

- They key to learning

- The manual for your brain

- An approach to communication, transformation and therapy

- The study of subjective experience

- The way to create your own future

- The toolkit for personal and organizational change

ORIGINS OF NLP

Give a man a fish and you can feed him for the day. Teach him to fish and you will feed him for the life. ~ Old Saying

In 1970's two geniuses - Richard Bandler and John Grinder, started on a quest to learn from the greatest therapists of all time. They studied Virginia Satir, Fritz Perls, Milton H. Erickson, Gregory Bateson etc. In every study they focused on decoding what these people were doing consciously and unconsciously while working with the clients. They called this process as Modeling.

Modeling is the study of behavior of excellence and chunking it down into imitable chunks or pieces. The therapist being modeled is referred to as "Exemplar" (not subject). The person modeling the exemplar is called a modeler. Hence the *modeler* uses several tools and techniques to *model* excellence from the *exemplar.*

The outcome of this process was then converted into simple step-by-step techniques or therapy models.

They also modeled the healing process of people who got cured of various psychological disorders – and it gave birth to techniques like Fast Phobia Cure, Submodalities work etc..

As the time progressed, many other people joined Richard and John in their studies and modelled exemplars from many other fields and added several more techniques under the umbrella of NLP.

Robert Dilts took on the project of modeling people who passed away long time ago and came up with "Strategies of Genius" series. Some of the people he modeled include – Jesus of Nazareth, Aristotle, Einstein, Walt Disney, Leonardo Da Vinci, Nikola Tesla etc.

These techniques were documented in several books. This new field of study and modeling was called Neuro-Linguistic Programming or NLP.

In this way NLP grew from just being a modelling tool to a toolbox.

NLP is no longer a tool, but a toolbox.

This toolbox contains hundreds of tools and techniques which are being used in coaching, counseling, therapy, sales, teaching, management and many more.

FOUR PILLARS OF NLP

A pillar is a structure on which a heavier and larger structure is standing. The pillar may look to be a small part of the overall structure. However, taking any pillar out weakens the structure. In this section we're going to discuss four such skills that are so essential to NLP, that absence of any of them weakens the effectiveness of the NLP work.

Rapport: Rapport here refers to the quality of your relationship with others as well as yourself. A major part of NLP is communication. And the communication required for change-work, isn't possible without rapport. Also, when you're working with clients, the change work isn't going to happen unless you ease the other person out through rapport building. Your rapport with your clients and important people in your life have to be A-one and your rapport with yourself has to be even better. Rapport here means the quality of your relationship with yourself. Do you accept yourself unconditionally? Or do you constantly criticize yourself over petty things?

Outcome thinking: In NLP you always think in terms of outcomes. For example, every session has a well-defined outcome(s). Even in a session, the outcome should be defined for each and every technique. We'll go into details of outcome thinking when we discuss well-defined or well-formed outcome criteria in this book.

Acuity: We're always communicating - even when we aren't actively talking. With practice, you can train your senses to be able to detect mood changes, signs of trance, signs of change, work being complete or not complete, etc. This ability is called sensory acuity. The more of the sensory acuity you have, the better you are in any field. In cricket, a master batsman is often able to tell if his bat is off by just couple of grams. Similarly, when you're working towards an outcome, you also need to have the acuity to tell whether you're on track or not.

Flexibility: Flexibility is the skill that one must know to exercise when things aren't working out. If someone doesn't have flexibility then they're bound to keep doing the same thing even when it's not working for them. You need flexibility when working towards the outcome of a session. You need good amount of flexibility when you're dealing with others. *If one thing is not working, try something else.*

CHAPTER 2
BELIEFS OF EXCELLENCE

You're aware that good and bad stuff happens to all of us. However, you see that some people are always happy no matter what happens to them. The hell may break loose on them and they seem to instantly bounce back. These are the people whom you can easily spot in the top rung of the society. They're entrepreneurs, change workers, trainers, coaches etc. These are the people whom you love to talk to when you are going through tough times in life.

These people are also termed as energizers. Here don't confuse them with famous motivators like Anthony Robbins, though he is certainly one of the best examples of such personality. I'm talking about people you can easily find in your relations, your friends, colleagues etc. They carry an aura of positivity.

For example, one such person I know - believes that everything happens for good. Even if something bad happens, she would hold the belief that eventually something good is going to come out of it. And surprisingly - it usually happens for her. She always emerges a victorious and better person from all the setbacks she encounters.

And then, there are people who are habitually depressed. No matter what life brings to them, they reframe it as bad or worse experience. Even if good things happen to them, they'll hold the belief, that the good times are short-lived and eventually, bad times are going to come upon them. Talking to these people isn't easy. They bring your energy down. Two words describe them best – Energy Vampires.

And I'm sure that you can find examples of such people in your life.

So, what is the difference? Life is neutral. Stuff happens to everyone. Good things and bad things happen to all of us. We all get up in the morning, hear good or bad news, get stuck in traffic, get red as well as green signals etc.

This is true for life as well.

BELIEFS OF EXCELLENCE

NLP has a set of powerful pre-suppositions, which are also called - Beliefs of Excellence.

By beliefs – I don't mean the religious or spiritual beliefs. They're some of helpful assumptions which you as an NLPer are recommended hold true in your life. These pre-suppositions are modeled after exceptional therapists who used to get results from all kind of clients.

You can accept them, challenge them or refine them. In my experience, holding them true has increased my level of happiness, reduced stress levels and made me more connected and flexible in life.

You don't have to believe in them, just act as if they were true and notice what happens.

PRE-SUPPOSITIONS

The word pre-supposition refers to an assumption - that you may not be able to prove logically - but you hold it true anyway.

Now, there may be some contexts where a particular pre-supposition isn't applicable. Hence, feel free to use your fine sense of judgement in such cases.

Here is a list of the main pre-suppositions that I've personally found helpful in my life:

1. Everyone has their own map of the world. The map isn't the territory.
2. People are more than their behaviors.
3. People make the best choices available to them at any point of time.
4. Meaning operates context-dependently.
5. Every behavior is useful in some context.
6. Behavior and change should be evaluated in terms of context and ecology.
7. We are always communicating. Or, we can't not communicate.
8. The meaning of the communication is the response you get.
9. All communication should increase choice.
10. The way we communicate affects perception and reception.
11. The person setting and controlling the frame of communication controls the action.
12. All processes should increase choice.
13. People have all the resources they need to succeed.
14. There is no failure, only feedback.
15. The person with most flexibility exercises has the most influence in the system.
16. Humans have the ability of one-trial learning.
17. Resistance indicates lack of rapport.
18. As response-able persons we can run our brain and control our results.
19. Every behavior has some unconscious positive intention.
20. Mind and body are one system.
21. The person controlling the frame of communication controls the action.
22. If someone can do it, anyone can do it.

Now, here is a brief explanation of each pre-supposition.

Everyone has their own map of the world. The map is not the Territory.

As discussed earlier, your brain uses five senses to take inputs from your surroundings. It then synchronizes and uses memory to create your unique single view of reality. That means that at no point you have a complete experience of reality. Also, brain cannot process the millions of bytes of information coming through the senses. It focuses on what is most important for you at the moment. For example, you're reading this book, but at the same time there are other things going around you, which your brain is ignoring as not much useful. For example, people walking past, honking in background etc. Hence, at no point you have a complete experience of reality. You always have a deleted view of reality. It's further distorted using your past memories and belief systems. Also, the phenomenon of generalization makes it easier to not pay attention to several things around you. Hence, you may switch lane hundreds of times while driving back to home and be completely oblivious of it. All you know is that you have to drive on particular side of the road, not hit the car in front of you and stop on red signal and go ahead on green signal. This is made possible through the process of generalization.

In short, you never have the completely pure experience of reality. You always have a individualized experience of reality – which represents reality for you – but is actually far away from reality. In NLP terms, you have your own map of the world.

And its role is the same as of an actual map – to help you navigate. A map can help you navigate through the territory. However, you shouldn't be attached to a particular map and treat it as the actual territory.

Just like you, others also have their own maps of the world. We as NLPers should respect everyone's map of the world.

It's important that you should consciously put efforts to keep your mental maps current – just like Google does with its territorial maps. Also, more important is to not judge others' maps or impose your maps on others.

When you're working with the clients – sometimes you may find that they're unable to get things which are so obvious to you. Or you may think that their choices are the dumbest in the world. That time, hold back from making judgements and reflect on this pre-supposition.

The other thing to note is, that it's not necessary that the more detailed maps are better. The map has to be useful. There have been times when even the most detailed maps have lead people astray.

People are more than their behaviors.

A saying goes like this - "Hate a person's deed, not the person".

People usually hold judgments about others based upon their behavior. But people are much more than their behaviors.

Also, remember that every behavior is useful in some context.

This pre-supposition has acceptance built into it. This is useful when you need to accept people, who have done something wrong to you in the past.

You can also use it upon yourself to let go of the guilt of previous misdeeds. One of my clients had guilt about few things he had done in past, that had hurt his family members. The family had forgiven him over the years, but he was still carrying guilt in his mind. I gave him this pre-supposition and asked him to think about all that he had done and repeat this pre-supposition till the feeling disappears. The client did it for one week and got liberated of the guilt he was carrying for several years.

People make the best choices available to them at any point of Time.

Most of the times we hear people cribbing about the decision that they made, opportunities they missed in past, the mistakes they made etc., where if they had behaved differently would have changed their lives forever. However, one has to realize that as the life is happening, there is no way for anyone to know what is going to happen in the next moment leave alone after a decade. We all consciously make decisions to the best of our knowledge, resources and perspectives we hold in our lives. As in stock market it's said that it's easier to look at a chart and see the trends one has missed to notice, but it's extremely difficult to predict what is going to happen at the rightmost edge of the chart.

Meaning operates context-dependently.

An example I give here – If someone says "I will kill you", means one thing if someone says it in a heated argument, and it means entirely another thing when two friends are joking and having great fun.

Every behavior is useful in some context.

Anger is one of the emotions which most of us know isn't useful in most of the situations. Many people permanently severe relationships in the heat of the moment. So, being angry isn't a useful behavior.

However, how about a soldier in battlefield? Is some amount of anger useful for him? How about killing someone? It's not a generally useful behavior. However, for a soldier on the battlefield, it is an useful behavior.

Every behavior has some unconscious positive intention.

This is a powerful pre-supposition. People are doing what they are doing because it's fulfilling some needs for them. For example, a smoker may be smoking because it gives him relaxation. Hence, in this case providing relaxation is the unconscious positive intention of smoking.

This is true for every behavior, no matter how much it's broken. For example, a thief is stealing because he wants to provide for his family.

Now, when we say the positive intention, we are referring to the positive intention for the person. There may not be any positive intention for others in the behavior. For example, a thief stealing money. He has positive intention for himself, i.e. to provide for himself and his family's need. But not for the person from whom he is stealing the money.

This is very useful when you want to make some behavior change in yourself. The theory is, that until and unless the unconscious positive intention is satisfied, the older behavior will come back. That's the main reason why the behavioral changes don't last long enough.

Mind and body are one system.

Your mind affects your body and vice versa. For example, when there are positive thoughts in mind, you feel lighter and energized. The posture is straight, head high and the walk is confident. However, when someone's thoughts are negative or depressive, the body feels heavy, the posture is slumped, head is low and the walk is as if they are dragging their feet.

The opposite is also true. When people have fever or low energy in body, the general thoughts are negative or depressive. And when the body is feeling light and is bursting in energy, the thoughts are fast paced, everything seems achievable, the general flow of thoughts is positive and happy.

Behavior and change should be evaluated in terms of context and ecology.

A particular behavior may be a good or bad in one context and absurd in another. For example, falling on floor while laughing, is good when you're in an informal environment. However, it isn't a good behavior in an executive meeting and strictly avoidable one in case you are attending a funeral.

Depending upon the context a behavior may or may not be ecological. Ecological means - whether something is good for you and the system/people around you.

Killing isn't an ecological behavior. However, killing in battlefield is an highly ecological behavior.

When someone comes to you for a change or you want to have some change in life, the first question to ask is – in which context is the change required? For example, say you want to have more free time. If you want to have more free time in your personal life then it's one thing. And if you want to have more free time in your professional life, then it's another thing. Both context will require different type of adjustments in life.

The next question to ask is – is it ecological? Depending upon the context a change may or may not be ecological.

For example, getting rid of the fear of height is desirable and ecological thing to have in general context. However, it's not ecological if one wants to be able to climb hundred story building and do a headstand on the boundary.

We are always communicating. Or, We Can't not communicate.

We don't communicate by words alone. We communicate through our bodies as well. For example, two youngsters travelling in same bus, may not be talking to each other initially, but they might be showing interest or disinterest in each other through their body language. Similarly, people communicate with each other through tone, eyes, smile or lack of it, and silence as well.

The meaning of the communication is the response you get.

Many times, you would have heard someone blaming other party of mistaking their words. I had a team mate who would often say, "I have been telling you this from day one, but you guys didn't listen to me properly, now we're in soup". Sometimes he might say, "No when I said <xyz>, I meant <abc>, you guys derived your own meaning"

This pre-supposition puts the responsibility of communicating the meaning squarely on the communicator. Again, this belief is mainly for you and not to hold others guilty of not communicating with you effectively. When you're in the same position as my team mate was, i.e. people are taking you for granted, or mis-interpreting your communication, you must think about how to communicate more effectively so that you communicate the right meaning to the receiver. Believe me, this one is going to save not only a lot of miscommunications and misunderstandings, and resulting fights, but enhance your image as well.

All communication should increase Choice.

This is a powerful pre-supposition. In NLP we believe in creating choices. Sometimes people talk in such a way that limits their choices. It's like my way or high way. This limits you from seeing the vast amount of inner resources in other people, and it strains the relationships.

Whenever you communicate, notice if there is any way you're limiting the choices that you and the other person has. For example, does having fun always means going to a movie for you and shopping for your spouse? In that case there isn't much choice available. It could be like – we can have fun today… so we can go to a movie, shopping, or that theme park, a long ride or can just be at home and cook something special and have it with nice wine over the dinner.

I know a manager whose conversation would be like:

(At 1:30 PM this manager would be waiting for an employee to return from lunch. As soon as he sees the employee has reached at his desk, the manager would walk over to the employee's desk.)

Manager: Hey… How are you doing? I need the root cause analysis of all the customer found bugs. I think there are 50 of them.

Employee: Ok. I think I can work on it. I'm busy right now.

Manager: Ok. Can you send it by 3 PM.

Employee: (hesitating) Hmmm let me see… I will try.

Manager: Ok. And, also I need to meet you regarding couple of outstanding issues. I have scheduled a meeting from 2PM to 3 PM..

Employee: (Inside his head: hmmm it is already 1:30 PM and then there is a meeting between 2-3 PM and by 3 he needs that report also… is this guy nuts! Does he want me to work here or not?)

As you see the employee doesn't have any choice when the manager is communicating with him. It's going to be no wonder if the employee moves out at the first opportunity.

The way we communicate affects perception and reception.

A mother saying, "NO" to a two year old in an authoritative tone or saying …"Nooooo" in a loving tone… or "No..no…no..no" in a rhythmic way means three different things, even though in all three instances the mother is saying No. The children often get confused when the mothers communicate same words in such ways. Initially they don't know how to react to them, but soon being fast learners, they pick up that the meaning of the words depends upon not only the words but the way they are said.

And we carry this throughout our lives. We not only value words but the way they are said.

The person setting and controlling the frame of communication controls the action.

The easiest way to think about this is the corporate meetings. For a long time, I used to hate people who would keep thinking about a future meeting in paranoid way. However, their effectiveness in the meetings was remarkable. By the time the meeting took place, they would have thought about most of the scenarios in which the conversation would go and what would they want out of the meeting. This gave them an upper hand than the ones who used to come unprepared. And ultimately, they would easily and effortlessly manipulate the meetings in such a way that most or at least their most significant wishes would get fulfilled.

Whenever you're going for a meeting, just think through what would you like to get out of it. Think about the items you would like to discuss and the questions you would like to ask. What questions people are going to ask you and how are you going to handle those questions to masterfully navigate the meeting in your favor.

All processes should increase choice.

This is in tune with NLP's core belief of increasing choices in lives.

We very often get caught up in the realm of duality. A client comes to a change worker, let's say a therapist, to get rid of the addiction of eating chocolate. The therapist immediately runs through a process, let's say a sub-modality change, which makes the chocolate look and feel like litter or garbage. The client before the process had no choice and after the process he again has no choice. Before, he couldn't resist chocolate and after the process, he couldn't help hating it.

A good therapist will allow the client to have more choices after the process just like he had more choices perhaps for eating a hamburger.

People have all the resources they need to succeed.

To succeed we need some internal resources. A person may be feeling lacking of a critical resource, let's say confidence in one context, for example, public speaking.

However, he would have experienced the confidence in playing soccer. So, he has confidence but in the context of soccer. Similarly, whatever other resources he needs could be found in some other contexts. In theory, he has all the resource he needs to succeed, but they may be scattered.

It's equivalent to having enough money to buy a new car or house, but that money being present in different bank accounts or in the form of other assets.

With NLP we can copy these resources from various contexts into the context in which the client wants to be successful.

There is no Failure, only Feedback.

We all have good and bad times. If there are successes then there are failures as well. When Thomas Edison failed thousand times in inventing the light bulb, he didn't say he has failed for a thousand times. He just said that he found thousand ways that the light bulb won't work.

Thus, he reframed all the failures into learning experiences or feedback.

Every time you fail, you get an important feedback of the process not working. And with enough required flexibility, you can easily do the course correction and move towards your goal.

The person with most flexibility exercises has the most influence in the System.

Most of the people in the world are inflexible. You take their core element away and they behave as if they're dysfunctional. This is the reason that people fear change. For example, when computers came in

India and public sector units were getting computerized, the government spent a huge amount in order to upgrade the workforce. However, most of the staff feared that since only handful of people are going to learn the computers, they will get humungous amount of work. This concern was valid. In other words they turned inflexible. Or the comfort zone kicked in. Still, few enterprising young at heart people took the chance and learned. These individuals saw rapid career growth. The inflexible ones had to accept voluntary retirement scheme as they no longer found themselves fitting in the new environment.

Life is about change. One needs to have a lot of flexibility in order to adapt to change. One of the best places to start is your career. Today's complex corporate environment offers a lot of challenges on day to day basis. One can exhibit flexibility and take advantages of as many learning opportunities as possible.

Humans have the ability of one-trial Learning.

This is a powerful pre-supposition to have when dealing with others. People learn phobias, fears or anxieties in few seconds in one particular incident, for example, getting frozen while trying to give a speech in assembly in fifth grade. And then, they carry this learning throughout their lives unless a powerful intervention like NLP Phobia Cure happens.

Just like they have learned the wrong behavior in one go, they can learn the right behavior also in one go. That means, unlike the belief that change takes time, the change can happen in an instant if the things are done in right way.

Resistance indicates lack of Rapport.

While working with clients, colleagues or friends, whenever you sense there's resistance, then it means that you need to work on rapport.

For a year the therapists have been keeping a cop out when the client couldn't see the results. They started telling the client that they (client) are resisting the treatment. And client gets baffled. Some clients try to use counter-logic like, "Hey, I have paid your fee which is so huge, to help me make this change. I have to be out of my mind to resist you." And to this, the therapists have a bigger cop out which goes like- "Well you may not be resisting me consciously. However, you have been resisting me unconsciously."

Well I would say – There are no resistant clients. There are inflexible therapists.

For your sake, when you find someone resisting you in personal or professional life, just fall back to rapport building. They aren't resisting you, they just don't trust you.

As response-able persons we can run our brain and control our results.

After reading this book and going through our NLP course, you don't have to become the football of other people's opinions or the victim of circumstances. You can easily control your brain and thus your results.

How to use these pre-suppositions?

While working with the clients, I generally give them one or two of these core beliefs to think over in the coming week. For example, for a person having communication issues with their spouse, I might tell them to think over – "All communication should increase choice" and

"Meaning of the communication is the response you get". They hold this belief in their head for the coming week. And invariably during the next week call they report remarkable improvement in their communication with their spouse leading to reduced conflicts and increased happiness.

Another way to use them, is to select one or two pre-suppositions each week and hold that pre-supposition true for that week. And by the time you exhaust all the pre-suppositions you will have expanded you mind and transformed your life and most probably positively impacted lives of others around you.

Every behavior has some unconscious positive intention.

Every substance addict knows that the substance is not good for their health. However, they still keep on repeating the behavior. If you go deeper, you'll find out that the person is doing this to fill some other need - for example, to suppress anxiety, or to avoid withdrawal symptoms etc. So, even the addiction has a positive intention for the other person by helping them avoid certain pain. Unless this positive intention is taken care of without the substance dependence - any change work is less likely to produce any results. That's the reason that many smokers quit smoking and have a relapse within few days.

Mind and body are one system.

Mind and body affect each other. If you're happy, your body also feels lighter and more energetic. You're able to get done more mentally as well as physically. However, if you're sad, you most likely feel lethargic and less energetic. Hence, the mind affects body. The converse is also true. This is very much evident when some part of your body hurts badly. You feel sadness, anger etc. Similarly, you can also change your mood by changing your body language. Next time when you're sad, just stand straight - as tall as possible by straightening your posture, pull your shoulders backwards and have a wide grin on your face.

The person controlling the frame of communication controls the action.

You might have experienced that you set up a meeting and someone else hijacks it and pushes his own agenda. In other words, you had set up a frame for the communication. However, later you lost control of the communication to the other person. And at the end of the meeting, the action items will reflect more of the other person's agenda than yours.

We have all internal RESOURCEs we need to succeed.

Internal resources are states like motivation, drive, persistence, hard-work etc. You have all of these resources. However, you may not be able to generate results in one of the areas for lack of one of these resources. For example, you may not be able to work on certain tasks in office, due to lack of interest or motivation. However, that doesn't mean you don't know how to motivate yourself or be interested. You certainly are interested and motivated to do several other things in your life. In NLP there are certain techniques which help us take a resource from one area of life and integrate it into another area where it's lacking.

There is no Failure, only feedback.

Many people beat themselves for failures in their lives. This creates a negative self-talk and makes them prone to more failures. However, successful people take the failures in more positive way by trying to learn from them. They take their lessons and don't repeat the mistakes in the next attempt. This improves their probability to succeed.

The person with most flexibility exercises the most influence in the System.

A person who is go-getter can get things done faster than others. They are viewed as valuable players despite their technical skillsets. Their inputs are valued more than the hardliners.

Resistance indicates lack of Rapport.

There are no resistant clients, only resistant therapists or coaches. And the reason for resistance is lack of rapport. If you find your client resisting the change work - just focus on getting the rapport back first and then proceed with the session.

If someone can do it, anyone can do it.

This comes from modelling. If one person can do something great, others can also do the same by breaking the process into small chunks and copying the other person's strategies as closely as possible.

CHAPTER 3
YOUR SENSES AND THE MAP OF THE WORLD

You have five senses to make sense of the world around you. You see through your eyes, hear through your ears, feel through your skin, smell through your nose and taste through your tongue.

Your senses take the data from the world around you and feed it to the brain through a series of electrical signals. Your brain then synchronizes this information to combine this into a single reality. It's like a super virtual reality system with five types of sensors. There are visual sensors which are just taking in visual information from their vicinity, there are mics to record sounds from their vicinity along with the direction and location from where the sounds are coming. Then there are sensors which take in kinesthetic information like the temperature, texture of things around it etc. Similarly, there are sensors for olfactory (smell) and gustatory (taste) information. These sensors are taking in information in a steady stream and feeding it into a central system. The task of the central system is to keep synchronizing this information. This is your brain in action.

The amount of data input is too huge. The brain cannot process the vast amount of data coming simultaneously through five senses. So, it focuses on what it considers is the most important information at the moment. To achieve this, it uses the processes called deletion, distortion and generalization to reduce the amount of input to manageable chunks. Hence, none of us have the real view of the reality. Or, we can say that all of us have a map of the reality – which is always few steps away from the reality.

Deletion: The prime directive of your mind is your survival. Due to this, the human brain has developed the habit of focusing on what it considers is the most important for its survival – an existential threat, or hunting for a meal to satisfy hunger. Today we know this skill as focusing. This skill enables the mind to cope up with the vast amount of information it's getting at any moment. You're reading this book, and going through the words line by line while your mind is absorbing the essentials of the content. However, as your mind is focusing on the activity of reading the book – there are other things happening around you which you aren't aware of. There may be people walking around you, or the humming of appliances, and your feet may be touching the floor or some other surface that your mind wasn't noticing until you read this sentence. The other information your mind might be ignoring is the temperature in the room, chirping of birds or sound of traffic in the background. At any moment the mind is focused on what it considers the most important for itself. And it conveniently deletes everything else. This is why sometimes you may place a pen and forget where you kept it just few minutes after.

Distortion: Your brain can make the information received better or worse by adding the meaning to it to make it compatible with your perceptions. This is why two persons read the same news in same newspaper and yet draw entirely different conclusions. For example, the news might be a politician X organizing a gala event to support a charity. Person A may consider this as a kind gesture, B may consider this a show off, C may consider this an election stunt and D may be neutral to it. The distortions may also happen at the level of language. A process may get converted to a noun. For example, the process of relating becomes relationship (I have a good relationship). Some other examples are justice, education, choice and cooperation. Your past memories also color the meaning of the information coming to your brain.

Generalization: The brain is busy analyzing the information coming to it and detecting patterns from it. This process is called generalization. The brain does this to avoid learning the same stuff again and again. This makes our lives easier. For example, people in every country drive on the same side, they stop on red and go on green, the door opens in one direction, the car drivers sit in seats located in front on right of left side depending upon the country etc. When people visit or shift to some other country where the doors open in opposite sides or people drive in opposite direction – there are several incidents of confusion in first few days. This is due to the generalizations already stored in the brain. After few days the brains learn new generalizations. Generalizations can also be harmful when a negative incident is generalized. A child is chased by a dog and the brain may generalize it into a belief that all dogs are dangerous or in some cases into a phobia. All phobias are overgeneralizations done by the brain. Similarly, some people have negative connotations attached to opposite gender due to some incidents that happened in the past and was generalized by brain.

YOU ARE NEVER EXPERIENCING REALITY

The brain as mentioned before deletes, distorts and generalizes the information coming to it. You're never experiencing the reality in its pure form. At best, your experience can be very close to reality, but still very far away from it. Or, we can say that you just have a rough map of the reality.

Also note, that no matter what happens your brain is always a little bit out of sync with reality - because by the time the information gets processed, the reality would have changed a bit. Hence, not only you have a map of the reality instead of the reality, it's slightly outdated map also.

The brain then uses the stored memories of similar events to decide the next action. This explains why people react differently to the same event.

Hence,

- All of us have a map of reality
- The map of reality isn't the same as reality
- Everyone reacts to their own map of the reality and not to the reality

MEMORY BANK

Also, when your brain takes in this information, it stores it in the memory to use it later. That is how while driving you know where you are and how long it will take to reach your destination.

There are two types of memories – **Short-Term** and **Long-Term**. A short-term memory is for immediate retrieval. Hence, when you stop at the red right - your short-term memory tells you that the red right is on and you're stopped. As soon as the signal turns green, you move pass the crossing and generally forget about waiting at the red light. However, the brain has stored in the information that you must stop at the red light in the long-term memory. Hence, across the world wherever you see red light - your brain will trigger reflex action and you will slow down to stop.

REPRESENTATIONAL MODES

Our five senses do much more than just experiencing the world. The brain uses the information coming from the five senses to code the incoming information in the form of memories. The information coming from the visual channel is stored as pictures. The information coming through the auditory channel is stored in the form of sound. The information coming from the kinesthetic channel are stored in the form of feelings. Similarly, the olfactory and gustatory information is stored in the form of smells and tastes.

The stored information is then retrieved from the memory whenever required. For example, think of a pleasant vacation that you undertook recently. If you cannot remember a vacation, then imagine one. And now think of a specific event in this vacation where you enjoyed it to the fullest. If several events come to your mind, just pick any one randomly. Now pay attention to the associated images coming to your mind. Are the images colored or black and white? Are they big or small? Are they near or far? Now, pay attention to any sounds you remember. Are these sounds loud or soft? Where are they coming from? Are they external or in your head? Is there any rhythm to the sounds? Now, pay attention to how you're feeling physically? What is the primary feeling? Where in your body are you feeling it? Is there any smell or taste also? How are you feeling as you are accessing this memory?

Where all this came from? You may not be necessarily on vacation as you are reading this book. Your brain retrieved it for you from its long-term memory bank as you read the previous paragraph. Also, the memory was internally coded or re-presented using the information from five senses in your brain. Due to this reason, the five senses are called *Representational Systems* or *Representational Modes* in NLP. These are also abbreviated as *RepSystems* or *RepModes.*

To summarize the five RepModes or Representation Systems are:

1. Visual (seeing)
2. Auditory (sounds)
3. Kinesthetic (feelings)
4. Olfactory (smell)
5. Gustatory (taste).

These are often notated as V, A, K, O and G respectively to avoid typing expanded forms.

Visual: You aren't only seeing what is happening outside but are also continuously creating visuals inside your head. The previous line would have created some sort of picture inside your head, just as this line has created picture of previous and this line. Think about your dream vacation – and notice the pictures that come to your mind.

You are continuously creating pictures as you think about the challenges, problems, solutions, daydream, imagine etc. When someone tells you about their dream vacation, you're creating pictures of whatever they're telling you about. If they tell you about a ferry ride with an orchestra playing – you create pictures of a ferry ride with orchestra playing to make sense of what the other person is saying. However, this is happening too fast for some people to notice.

Whatever you are seeing now will be stored in the brain in the form of pictures. Whenever you recall this memory – the brain will retrieve these pictures for you. Think about a pleasant holiday you had in past and notice how the images of things you saw came to your mind. What is the favorite dress you wore on that vacation? Did this bring the picture of that dress to your mind? Did this also bring the pictures of the occasion(s) on which you wore it?

Your mind responds to the pictures you hold in your mind. If you're holding positive pictures – the mind accepts these as commands and creates success in the areas wherever you are holding positive pictures. Holding positive pictures of health and well-being is the formula for wellness. On the other hand, if someone is holding pictures of failures, embarrassment etc., the mind takes those as commands as well. No one has held negative pictures in the mind and then surprised themselves with huge success.

Top athletes and peak performers have realized the power of holding positive images in their heads. The athletes continuously train their minds by visualizing themselves pushing harder and harder in their efforts and breaking their own records. Further, there are visualizations for tacking more specific areas like starting off in a race, finishing the race, or holding and swinging the golf club in specific way, playing in the zone etc.

Exercise:

- Think about an area in your life where you would like to generate better results
- What are the primary images you are holding about this area. Do you have more images of challenges and failure?
- Now create a new image of how the success and peak performance in this area will look like
- Relax and hold this picture in your mind several times a day. Notice the difference in this area every week. Change the visualization as required. Do this until you realize the goal.

Auditory: Auditory means two things – the sounds that you're hearing and that will be stored in memory. And the sound that your internal chatter is continuously making inside your head.

The sounds which you are hearing right now are processed and stored in the memory as sounds. Later on when you recall this memory, the same sounds will be retrieved from the memory. Continuing with the same vacation as in the previous section – think of the memory again. As this memory comes to your mind – are there any sounds associated with it? Do you remember the waiter taking an order? Do you remember the most pleasant sound you heard during that vacation? Did this sound bring the face of someone or the scene of some place to your mind?

Your internal chatter is also continuously creating sounds inside your head. The quality of your life hugely depends upon the quality of this internal dialogue. The peak performers have positive internal dialogue. The low performers have negative self-talk. This shows in the body posture and energy levels. Top players and athletes have recognized it a long time back and it has popularized the use of affirmations.

An affirmation is a positive statement to dampen and eliminate the negative self-talk. For example, if someone is struggling with weight issues – they can create affirmations like:

- I am continuously working towards my goal of ideal weight
- It is January 31, year xxxx and I have total weight of xx kilograms.
- I eat healthy meals when I am hungry

Exercise:

- Think of an area of life where you want to generate positive results but aren't able to.
- What is your primary self-talk about this area?
- Create some affirmations for yourself in this area.
- Repeat these affirmations for a week and notice the difference.
- Continue repeating these affirmation for two more weeks.

Kinesthetic: The kinesthetic representational system is made up of external and internal feelings of touch and bodily awareness. You're feeling the temperature and surfaces all the time. Your body keeps sending the signals to brain if it's too hot or too cold to take the necessary action. The body is also sending signals about the internal feelings e.g. the butterflies in stomach to the brain. The emotions also form part of kinesthetic representational mode. The emotions manifest in the form of physical sensations. You feel happiness and loss in heart. One of these is light and other weighs heavy on heart. You can recall experiences when you or someone else had headache due to a lot of stress. When a memory gets stored, the sensation of hotness or coldness is also stored in the memory. Being with the same memory of a pleasant vacation, recall a special moment from that vacation. What is the most memorable feeling? Can you recall the temperature? If it was a walk – can you recall how did your feet feel while walking on the sand or that surface?

Olfactory: This system consists of remembered and created smells. The olfactory system isn't much developed in humans. The ants however are perfect examples which live their lives based upon olfactory sense. However the olfactory system is recognized to be most powerful anchor or trigger for old memories. You may be forty, fifty or sixty year old – but a specific aroma of your childhood favorite dish can send you back to the memories of your grandmother's house when you were five year old.

Gustatory: This system consists of remembered and created tastes. Just like olfactory this sense isn't highly developed. However, it plays great role in our lives. A huge number of people are self-proclaimed foodies due to this sense only. Children are addicted to pizza, chips, junk food etc. due to gustatory sense itself. Similarly, we know whether a food is rotten or milk isn't suitable to be consumed by the gustatory + olfactory sense.

The processing of representational modes can be summarized as below:

Sensory interaction with the environment	Internally represented as:	Information constructed or recalled as: (Subjective Experience)
Visual – Eyes	Pictures	Visuals, pictures
Auditory – Ears	Sounds	Sounds
Kinesthetic – Skin/Body	Feelings	Sensations/Feelings
Olfactory – Nose	Smell	Smells
Gustatory – Tongue	Taste	Taste

In most of NLP we mainly focus on visual, auditory and kinesthetic representational modes. The olfactory and gustatory aren't developed as much in humans as the other three modes. The olfactory and gustatory are sometimes clubbed under kinesthetic representational mode itself.

REPRESENTATIONAL MODE AND COMMUNICATION

In NLP we believe that – *You can't not communicate*. That means you're always communicating at subconscious level. The way a person communicates describes what is going on in their head.

For example, if you present an idea to a person the person may respond in one of the following ways:

1. "Looks good" – visual processing
2. "Sounds good" – auditory processing
3. "Feels great" – kinesthetic processing
4. "It's a fresh idea" – olfactory processing
5. "Oh! What a spicy idea" – gustatory processing
6. "I understand it" – None of the VAKOG.

Hence, we always give away information about which representational mode we're accessing in our heads – visual, auditory, kinesthetic, olfactory, gustatory or none of these. These give away words are called *predicates* or *process words*.

It's a powerful weapon of influence. If a person tells you, that they *cannot see a point* in your idea – they're processing information visually. It's in your benefit to show them the presentation that you prepared for the idea or draw a diagram to make them *see* the idea. On the other hand, it would be a mistake to tell them something like – "Oh okay, let me explain the idea to you in more detail". For the needed input through is visual channel and you're addressing his auditory channel. This is going to break rapport with the person. Matching a person's representational modes and providing information to the person in the same representational mode is a key influencing skill. It leads to better rapport and more understanding.

PRIMARY REPRESENTATIONAL SYSTEM

As you know, your brain is a busy machine. It's always busy taking and processing information from the world around you using your five senses and synchronizing it into a single reality.

However, your senses or your representational modes aren't equally developed. With time one of the representational modes emerges as the primary representational mode. This explains why some people find it difficult to visualize what happened few days ago while others are able to visualize an event that happened ten years ago. A highly visual person codes most of the information visually. Does that mean that they don't store sound and feelings? No. It just means that the amount of visual information stored is far higher than the other two modes. A highly auditory person stores more memory in terms of sounds and noises. They store visual and kinesthetic information to lesser extent. Similarly, a highly kinesthetic person stores information more in terms of feelings than visual or auditory information.

A study has shown that 60% of people process information visually, 20% process information auditorily and 20% process information kinesthetically.

The above fact can explain some of the difficulties you might be having in putting your point across. For example, if you're a primary visual person and are giving a presentation. If you aren't aware of representational modes, you will tend to use the visual language. In this process you will end up catering to just 60% of the audience or unintentionally neglecting 40% of the audience.

SIGNIFICANCE OF PRIMARY REPRESENTATIONAL MODE

The primary representational mode is highly significant. Think of it as the comfort zone of your brain. It will use it more heavily than other senses for getting things done, overcoming the challenges, entertainment, etc. Now, it doesn't mean that the brain won't use other senses at all – it will use more than one sense for getting everything done, but will use the primary representational mode more heavily.

For example, your entertainment choices depend upon your primary representational mode. If your primary RepMode is visual - you would tend to gravitate towards visual activities like watching movies, videos on Internet, going through presentations to understand new concepts etc. Your auditory friend would prefer to listen songs, audio books etc. The kinesthetic friend will tend to learn by doing, engage in sports which are highly kinesthetic or go for a walk to calm down.

You'll also select your careers accordingly. If someone's career doesn't align with their preferred representational mode, they may feel challenges in it and may feel burned out more frequently. For example, most of the movie actors are highly kinesthetic people, you will see them happily dancing, or even crying spontaneously on talk shows without feeling embarrassed. However, they're supposed to impress. They are supposed to dress in clothes that are visually appealing but kinesthetically uncomfortable. They have to follow strict diet plans to maintain their looks. This leads to building of emotional discomfort. Hence, no wonder many of them burn out very fast and their careers are over – and in some cases take up addictions.

You even dress according to your primary representational mode. If you're a visual person - you tend to prefer the looks over comfort. But if you're a kinesthetic person - you would prefer comfort and looks will come second in your category. One of my friends keeps wearing shirts and trousers which he purchased many years ago. He does it till the thread gives away. He then uses them as night clothes. However, he isn't a frugal person. He is earning very well and spends a lot on gadgets etc. He even has a good collection of clothes. Still, he prefers old clothes over new ones because as the cloth wears out the thread becomes softer and feels better.

USING THE PRIMARY REPRESENTATIONAL MODE TO INFLUENCE OTHERS

The discussion so far about primary representational mode is a powerful information in your hands, which you can use for influencing others, isn't it? Suppose you want to influence an important colleague, your boss, potential investor or someone special. Knowing their primary representational mode will help you be more effective with that person. An expensive picture frame as a gift to a kinesthetic person isn't going be as effective as a gift coupon to his favorite sports club. Similarly, an auditory person will be thrilled more by a music collection of his favorite singer than by a Disney Land ticket. A visual person is more likely to enjoy a laser show, a scenic ride or a movie with special effects etc.

Let us see how can you find out someone's primary representational mode.

FINDING OUT SOMEONE'S PRIMARY REPRESENTATIONAL MODE

It's very easy to decipher someone's primary representational mode. Just talk to them for couple of minutes and notice the kind of words they use.

Visual people use more visual words and phrases, for example - look, see, perspective, birds eye view etc. while talking.

Auditory people use more auditory words and phrases like – sounds good, harmony, rings a bell, call in etc. while talking.

In the same way, kinesthetic people tend to use words and phrases like – feels good, having a handle on issue, grasping a concept etc.

For example, if you present a brilliant idea to three persons with different primary representation modes, the visual person may reply that it "looks good", the auditory person may say that it "sounds good", and the kinesthetic person may respond that it "feels good".

Here are some more ways you can make out a person's primary representational mode. As mentioned previously, in NLP we focus on visual, auditory and kinesthetic representational modes. The olfactory and gustatory senses are never developed enough to become primary representational mode. For this reason this section omits olfactory and gustatory modes.

Visual:

A visual person breathes from upper part of their chest. Their eyes are more in the upper half as they're accessing the visual images while talking. Also, since they're accessing images and describing them they speak too fast. Remember the saying – "A picture is worth a thousand words"? Hence, they speak more and describes they experience in as much detail as possible. That means they need to pack more words in each breath. So, their breathing is shallow and fast. They seldom do belly breathing. If you observe, they seem to be breathing from the upper part of their chest and you can clearly make out their shoulders moving as a result of breathing from upper chest. Also since they're describing a picture, their hand movements will be angular, as if tracing shapes or the frame of picture. They'll tend to use words like see, watch out, look, perspective, focus etc. In meetings they would prefer presentations with a lot of pictures, logos, colorful fonts, flow charts, diagrams, etc. You literally have to show them the idea for them to be able to process it properly.

Auditory:

The auditory person breathes from mid chest. Their speech is rhythmic and paced. It's neither too fast nor too slow. Their gestures are balanced and include touching face. When they think about something they might lean on to the table or arm rest and put their hand on their face in telephone position. They look down and to the left very often as they're having a lot of internal dialogue. While talking they would use words like hear out, listen, ask, in-tune, in harmony etc. They doesn't like presentations as they distract them. You have to talk about your idea for them to be able to process it. In presentations, they prefer bullet points over flashy pictures and diagrams.

Kinesthetic:

A kinesthetic person has to experience things before they talk. Hence, their speech is slow. Their breathing is deep and slow and very often they breathe from their belly. They look down to the right very often as they're accessing feelings. Their gestures are rhythmic and include touching their chest. They use words like feel, touch, grasp, handle the situation, etc. They prefer physical books and documents over the presentations.

As mentioned in the beginning of the section, we can find out someone's representational mode by listening to their talk. The language does more than giving away a person's representational mode. Your language at any point of time points to what is going inside your head through giveaway words. These giveaway words in NLP are called Predicates or Process Words.

PREDICATES OR PROCESS WORDS

In our last section we discussed, that while talking you automatically choose words based upon what's happening inside your brain. In NLP these are called predicates or process words.

When people are talking, they're continuously accessing visual, auditory, kinesthetic, olfactory or gustatory information in their heads. If you pay attention to their language - you can make out what they're doing in their heads. For example, a friend may come to you and say, "Hey, I have got a bright idea, which looks very promising for ....". In this example, "bright" and "looks" keywords, in the friend's casual language are giving away the clue that he's visualizing bright images of the idea in his head.

Another friend may come to you and tell – "Listen we need to talk about the new proposal. I would like to hear your side and then we can discuss it further and take a call." Here the friend has used the words – listen, talk, hear, discuss and call, which means he's processing things auditorily.

And if the friend were processing it kinesthetically, he would have said something like – "Hey, I would like to go through the new proposal. I would like to get your inputs and then we can go through all pros and cons and make a decision."

Wouldn't it be nice if you had a list of the words for each area? Below is a list of some of common predicates in English language associated with each representational system.

Visual

See, Picture, Perceive, Notice, Look, Show, Appear, Clear, Pretty, Colorful, Hazy, Observe, Flash, View, Vista, Horizon

Auditory

Sound, Hear, Discuss, Listen, Talk, call on, Quiet, Pronounce, Remark, Resonate, Harmony, Shrill, Oral, Inquire, Noisy, Loud, Outspoken, Articulate, Scream, Whisper, Mention

Kinesthetic

Feel, Relax, Grasp, Handle, Stress, Pressure, Grip, Warm, Rush, Firm, Euphoric, Smooth, Clumsy, Rough, Hard, Clammy, Touch, Calm, Burning, Stinging

Olfactory/Gustatory

Smell, Fragrant, Stink, Reek, Aroma, Pungent, Fresh. Bland, Stale, Fresh, Bitter, Sour, Sweet, Acrid, Musty, Salty, Nutty, Delicious, Salivate, Spoiled, Sniff, Smokey, Bitter pill, Fishy

Unspecified (which don't fall in any of the categories above)

Think, Decide, Understand, Know, Develop, Prepare. Activate, Manage, Repeat, Advise, Indicate, Consider, Motivate, Plan, Anticipate, Create, Generate, Deduce, Direct, Achieve, Accomplish, Initiate, Conclude

PREDICATE PHRASES

Similar to Predicate Words, people use some phrases also which point to the brain activity.

Visual:

An eyeful, appears to me, beyond a shadow of doubt, bird's eye view, catch a glimpse of, clear cut, clear view, dim view, eye to eye, flashed on, get a perspective, get a scope on, hazy idea, horse of a different color image, in light of, in person, in view of, mental picture, mind's eye, naked eye, paint a picture, photographic crystal, plainly seen, pretty as a picture, see to it, short sighted, showing off, sight for sore eyes, snap shot, staring off in space, take a peek, tunnel vision, under your nose.

Auditory:

Be all ears, be heard, blabber mouth, clear as a bell, clearly expressed, call on, call off, describe in detail, an earful, express yourself, give an account of, give me your ear, grant me an audience, heard voices, hidden messages, hold your tongue, idle talk, inquire into, key-note speaker, loud and clear, make music, manner of speaking, outspoken, pay attention to, power of speech, purrs like a kitten, rap session, rings a bell, state your purpose, tattle-tale, to tell the truth, tongue-tied, tune in/tune out, unheard of, voice an opinion, word for word.

Kinesthetic:

All washed up, back to square one, be felt, boils down to, catch on, chip off the old block, come to grips with, connect with, control yourself, firm foundation, floating on thin air, get a hold of, get a handle on, get in touch with, get the drift of, hand in hand, hands on, hang in there, heated argument, hold it, hold on, know-how, lay the cards on the table, light headed, make contact, moment of panic, pain in the neck, pull some strings, sharp as a tack, slip through, slipped my mind, smooth operation, start from scratch, stiff upper lip, throw out, tap into, turn around

Olfactory/gustatory:

Smell a rat, bitter relationship.

Unspecified/Digital:

Aware of, creative option, doesn't compute, factor in, get an account of, hash it out, the bottom line, new knowledge.

INFLUENCING WITH PREDICATES OR PROCESS WORDS

These process words or predicates are a strong weapon in your arsenal. The predicates serve as a window to the person's mind. You can use these in several ways.

• Firstly, you can use these words to calibrate someone's primary representational mode. A visual person uses more of visual predicates, and auditory uses more of auditory predicates and a kinesthetic person uses more of kinesthetic keywords.

• Secondly, when someone is talking to you and unconsciously giving away their process words in specific order – say first visual, then kinesthetic followed by auditory. Then using similar process words in same order builds faster rapport and more understanding. This puts you in the control of your conversation.

• Thirdly, it gives you a great weapon of influence. For example, if your potential client says that he is unable to see the benefits of your product clearly, then it's time to pull out a presentation with nicely formatted product pictures and comparison diagrams with the competitor products. If the client says that it doesn't ring a bell – then it's time to put the presentation away and talk about the product such that it rings a bell that is loud and clear.

OBSERVE A FRIEND EXERCISE

- Build rapport with a friend.

- Pay close attention to the choice of words. Are these visual, auditory, kinesthetic, olfactory, gustatory or unspecified

- Notice the rhythm and pace of the speech.

- How are their hand gestures? Are they angular or are the hands just relaxed? What is the correlation between the hand gestures and the representational mode they're talking about?

- Observe the body posture. Is it upright or relaxed? Where are they breathing from? Notice the correlation between the verbal representational mode and the breathing space.

Pacing representational mode is a very good way of building rapport.

Pacing and Leading Representational Mode Exercise:

- In above exercise, verbally pace the friend's representational mode. Use visual words if they are using visual words. Use auditory words if they are using auditory words etc. Notice the quality of the conversation.

- Disagree with the friend while pacing the representational mode. Notice the quality of conversation and mutual respect.

- Agree with the friend while pacing the representational mode and notice the quality of rapport.

• Now change your representational mode and notice if the friend follows. For example, if both of you were talking in visual modality, you may want to lead with – "How does all this sound like?" or "How do you feel about it?".

EYE ACCESSING CUES

You're always communicating. Even when you aren't talking actively - your body is giving out the signals about what's going on inside you. In the beginning days of NLP, the founders of NLP discovered that the eyes of a person move corresponding to what they're doing inside their head even when they aren't communicating externally. For example, Richard Bandler and John Grinder would ask an audience of 300 to remember an image from past and all eyes would go up to the left (of the audience). And then they would ask the audience a question which required them to create a new image, and all eyes would go up to the right. Your eyes are wired to the brain. And when your brain creates images or remembers an old song - different areas of the brain get lighted and the associated nerves also get activated. This activity in the brain produces corresponding movement in the eyes. Richard and John called it eye accessing cues.

The eye accessing cues are so powerful that these are used in interviews and interrogations to detect whether a person is speaking truth or not. For example, if one of your employees is late to office and you ask the reason for them being late. Suppose they say that they got stuck in traffic – pay close attention to their eyes. If the eyes move up to their left, then they're accessing the memory of the event that actually happened. However, if the eyes move up to their right, then they're creating images of something that didn't happen.

Below are the patterns for right handed (i.e. right hemisphere dominating) people. These patterns are sometimes reversed in left handed people and very rarely in right handed as well.

Eyes Up and Left: Remembered imagery (V^r)

Eyes Up and Right: Constructed imagery and visual fantasy (V^c)

Eyes Lateral Left: Remembered sounds, words, tape loops (A^r)

Eyes Lateral Right: Constructed sounds and words (A^c)

Eyes Down and Left: Internal dialogue, or inner self-talk (A^{id}).

Eyes Down and Right: Feelings, both tactile and visceral (K).

Eyes Straight Ahead, but Defocused or Dilated: Quick access of almost any sensory information; but usually visual.

Here is the pictorial representation of eye accessing cues:

As you see the chart, it portrays the person as you look at them.

Now, don't take it as a hard and fast rule that the eye accessing cues are going to always happen in the depicted manner. Several people are cerebrally reversed. For them the sides would reverse. The same is true for many left-handed people. For some people, the eye movements are very subtle and you'll have to pay very close attention to their eye pupils.

However, don't take the eye accessing cues at face value i.e. don't brand a person a liar if their eyes go towards the right side. For bi-lingual person the eyes may move all over the place as they trie to translate what is said and their response in their mind. Also, we cannot predict the eye accessing positions if a person is nervous.

There can also be anomalies due to Synesthesia, where the senses are mixed up. So a person may look right up (i.e. visual created) and say, "I feel …".

Use eye accessing cues discreetly. Don't stare into someone's eyes. Many people don't appreciate prolonged eye contact or others staring into their eyes. It makes them non-conformable. It doesn't mean that they're underconfident. It's most probably a programming from childhood, which has now become a comfort zone.

Let us now go through an exercise which will help you practice eye accessing cues.

MAPPING EYE ACCESSING PATTERNS EXERCISE

Work with a friend, ask the friend to just think the answers to following questions in his head and not say them aloud.

Visual remembered: Recalling pictures or images.

See the color you most favored as a child.

See the color of the bedroom of your childhood home.

See yourself, today morning. How did you brush your teeth?

Visual constructed: Making up pictures you have never seen.

Imagine yourself with green hair.

Imagine your bedroom walls painted in golden color.

Can you imagine top half of a tiger with bottom half of an elephant?

Auditory remembered: Recalling sounds or voices previously heard.

Listen to your favorite song. What does it sound like?

Which is louder, your door bell or your telephone?

Listen again to the very last statement I made.

Auditory constructed: Creating new sounds.

Hear your grandmother singing in Chinese.

What will your voice sound like in 10 years?

Hear me sounding like I had Donald Duck's voice.

Kinesthetic: Emotions, feelings, sensations.

Feel yourself rubbing your hand over a very fine fur coat.

Feel your love for the person you love the most.

What does it feel like to walk barefoot on a sandy beach?

Auditory Digital: Internal talk.

Talk to yourself about what you really want out of life.

What is something you continuously tell yourself?

What are your thoughts about this book/article/workshop?

CHAPTER 4
TAKING CHARGE OF YOUR BRAIN: SUBMODALITIES

In this chapter we are going to build on the concept of the representational mode and take it to the next level through the concept of Submodalities.

The concept of Submodalities is one of the most important discoveries in the field of NLP. Many techniques in NLP are based on this concept. From removing bad memories to belief change - you can do almost anything if you get this concept right.

WHAT GIVES MEANING TO MEMORIES?

It has been observed that not all memories are stored in your brain equally. For example, some memories are neutral memories, while others have some emotional charge associated with them. Memories which invoke emotions, either good, bad or mixed, are called the memories with emotional charge.

It has been found that the brain stores memories with a particular emotional charge in same way. For understanding the concept just think of a memory that is neutral for you and notice the pictures and their color. Now, think of a memory that you cherish - and notice the picture and the color. Third, think of another memory which is a bad memory for you. Notice the picture and color. If you're like most of the population - the first picture of the neutral memory might be a small or medium sized black & white picture. The other two pictures would be colored and quite big and without border. Now, pay attention to the location of the pictures of good and bad memories. You might notice that they tend to be on opposite sides or at least bit far from each other. For example, if the good memory is to your right, the bad memory would be to the left. That means the brain is following some sort of patterns to organize things and give them a meaning. To further convince yourself, think of some more memories and notice the picture locations, sizes and colors. You'll notice that good memories consistently show up on the same side as other good memories and the bad memories show up on the opposite side along with other bad memories.

The more colorful and bigger the picture, the more emotional charge it invokes. And the smaller and less colorful the picture, the lesser emotional charge it evokes. Now, take one of the bad memories and drain it of all color so that it becomes black and white. You'll notice that the intensity of the emotional charge disappears and you will feel liberated. This is the time to formally introduce Submodalities.

What Are Submodalities?

Submodalities are the finer distinctions associated with each modality, that encode and give meaning to our experiences. These are qualities of a modality.

For example, a picture in memory can have some qualities like color, brightness, size etc. Also, it can be a 2D – a flat picture like the one we keep in an album or it can be a three-dimensional movie. The picture also has a location associated to it. It can be inside the head or out of the head. Further if it's outside the head, it can be near or far away. Also imagine there's a vertical center line in front of you which divides your vision into two parts – left and right. The picture can be either to the right or left of this line. You can either see yourself in the picture, in which case it's called dissociated, or you may be experiencing it as if you're there in the picture – in which case you can see everything else but not yourself. In the latter case, it's called associated picture. These are all Submodalities of visual modality.

It's been seen that if you make a memory associated, bigger, brighter and more colorful the emotional charge associated with it increases. Whether it made you feel good or bad, your feeling will multiply manifold. Depressed people make their negative memories big, bright and more colorful. They get fully associated with them. And at the same time, they make their good memories far away, smaller, black and white, and dissociate from them. This makes their lives miserable. Successful people on the other hand make their good memories bigger, brighter, more colorful and become fully associated with them. They reduce the sizes of bad memories, make them black and white, 2D, push them far away and become fully dissociated from them. This increases their happiness quotient. Both persons might be living under similar circumstances in the same neighborhood, but one would be miserable and may be visiting doctors and the other would be leading a happy enjoyable life.

We also hear internal sounds. Whenever you're accessing a memory and thinking about what someone said, you're replaying their voice in your head. Similarly, when you're remembering your favorite song, you're playing the sound inside your head. This sound will have some qualities associated with it like volume, rhythm, tempo, pitch, location etc. When you're listening to a voice inside your head, it can be your voice or someone else's – mostly an authority figure. People with self-esteem issue often report having a continuous inner voice inside their head that keeps telling them that they aren't enough. It's either to the left or to the right. Some of these are very loud, while others are soft. Sometimes, there's just silence.

The feelings, internal or external also have qualities associated with them. Mind and body are connected. When mind is feeling good and happy – the body also feels light. And when the mind is foggy or sad, you feel that in the body too. In NLP we're concerned about where do you feel the feeling in body and we work through the Submodalities of the feeling in body. For example, if you feel love for someone – you feel it in the heart area. Similarly, in case of breakup there is sinking feeling in the heart area. In exams, you felt butterflies in your gut. Notice that for any feeling to be felt in body, there has to be some movement. If I stomp on your foot again and again, you'll feel pain. However, if I stomp on your foot once but don't take my foot off, then you'll feel pain initially, but after some time your body will adjust to it and you won't feel the pain anymore. A feeling is felt when it's moving. Sometimes people tell me that they have a knot in their solar plexus or throat which isn't moving, but they can feel it. I ask them if it's vibrating – and most of the time the answer is yes. Sometimes I tell them to rotate their hands in circles in forward, backward or sideways directions while paying attention to the knot and notice in which direction the knot is moving.

NLP approaches the problems in different way. The therapists would see a person going through frustration and ask – "why are you frustrated?", and this would go on for years. In NLP we ask, where do you feel the frustration in your body? And what is the starting point and ending point. Once you have the direction, you can effectively tackle it within few minutes using "Spinning feeling technique".

Table 1 gives a list of Submodalities and the questions to elicit them.

Table 1

VISUAL

B/W or Color	Is the picture color or black and white?
Near or Far	Is it near or far?
Bright or Dim	Is it brighter or dimmer than normal?
Location	Where is the image located in the space? Point to the direction in which they are located?
Size of Picture	Is it big or small?
Associated/Dissociated	Are you associated or dissociated? **If the person has no concept of association/dissociation:** *Do you see yourself in the picture or just the other things around you?*
Focused/Defocused	Is it focused or defocused?
Focus (Changing/steady)	Is the focus changing or steady?
Framed or Panoramic	Does it have frame around it?
Movie or Still	Is it a still picture or a movie? **If movie:** *Is the movie faster or slower than normal?*
2D or 3D	Is it 2D or 3D?

AUDITORY

Location	Where is it located?
Direction	Could you point to the direction from which the sounds are coming?
Internal/External	Is it internal sound or external?
Volume (Loud/soft)	Is it loud or soft?
Speed (Fast/slow)	Is it fast or slow?
Pitch (high/low)	Is it high pitch or low pitch?
Rhythm?	Does it have a rhythm to it?

KINESTHETIC

Location	Where is the feeling located inside your body?
Size	What is the size of the feeling?
Shape	What is the shape of the feeling?
Color	What is the color of the feeling?
Intensity	How is the intensity – strong or weak?
Direction of Movement	In which direction is it moving? Could you locate the start and end points of the feeling?
Fast or Slow	Is the movement fast or slow?
Vibration?	Does it have vibration?

Hot/cold	Is it hot or cold?
Pressure (high/low)	Is the pressure high or low?
Texture (rough/smooth)	Is it rough or smooth?
Heavy/Light	Is it light or heavy?

ELICITING SUBMODALITIES EXERCISE

Here is an introductory exercise which helps you to start working with Submodalities. This exercise is called eliciting Submodalities. Select a pleasant memory for this exercise.

You can do this alone or in a group of two if you have a partner. It's better to do this with a partner for first few iterations. If you have a partner then designate one of you as A and the other as B.

1. Without asking for content. B asks A to recall a pleasant memory. A recalls a memory.
2. B uses questions in column 2 of Table 1 to find out how the memory is stored – e.g. is it black & white or color, is the picture near or far etc.
3. B notes down the responses.
4. A and B interchange roles.

This process is called eliciting Submodalities.

Now, just play around a little bit with the memory.

Notice the color of the image. And also notice how do you feel when you think of this memory. Now, if it's colored then slowly make it black and white. Notice how it feels. You might notice that just changing the color neutralizes the good memory. Now, restore the original colors, and notice what happens. Did you get the original emotional charge back? Now make it more colorful, bigger, brighter and 3D. And notice what happens. For most of us it increases the intensity of the feeling. Now, keep increasing the brightness till it becomes so bright that you start losing the details. You would probably have lost the feelings again. So again, reduce the brightness to just the right levels so that you have the original feelings back.

POWER OF SUBMODALITIES

Submodalities give meaning to the feelings. Events that happen around you are neutral. Two people emerge out of a car crash. One of them forgets the memory after a year and the other get phobia of going on the road. Everyone reads news of plane crashes. However, I have heard about a case where a person got phobia of flights on reading one famous plane crash.

We store likes and dislikes also at different places in mind. Think of someone you like and notice where the picture shows up and how does it look like. Now think of one more person you like and notice the similarities in both pictures. Repeat this with two persons whom you dislike. Notice the similarities between the pictures of disliked persons. They would show up at different location than the persons whom you like. Repeat the exercise with food items, places etc.

RELEASE A BAD MEMORY

Now you're ready to move to the next level. Here you'll learn how to use Submodalities to neutralize a bad memory. A bad memory is nothing but a memory with emotional charge attached to it. If we get rid of the emotional charge – all that is left out is the recall of an event.

Again, sit in a group of two. One of you is person A and the other is person B.

1. Without asking for content, B asks A to recall a mildly bad memory. A recalls a memory.
2. B elicits the Submodalities using Table 1 and notes down the responses to each question.
3. Now B guides A to change the Submodalities one by one to weaker opposite of it. E.g. change the colored memory to black and white, big picture to small one etc. Make sure to do this step little faster and repeat couple of times.
4. Break state.
5. Test: B asks A to try to recall memory and report how does A feel.

If the techniques worked then A shouldn't feel any emotional charge upon recalling the memory. It should appear as a neutral even. In some cases, A may even have difficulty in recalling the event.

GETTING RID OF FOOD CRAVINGS

Is there any food you're really crazy about but want to get rid of the craving? Mapping across Submodalities can be the solution.

Mapping across Submodalities means taking two experiences and changing the Submodalities of one of the experiences to those of the other. For example, you can change the Submodalities of the things you crave for, to those of the things that you're neutral about. And this will transform your craving response into neutral response.

Use this technique for a food craving that you have and would like to have control over it. Don't worry, it won't take away the enjoyment that you have from having that food. It'll merely give you more options.

Food craving is something that very few people have any control over. A client of mine couldn't control herself the moment she saw a chocolate. "Death by Chocolate" was her favorite. She was so addicted to it that she was having it almost every day while returning from office. This was impacting her pocket as well as her health. Also, she had just started her job with a small company. Hence, the financial impact was significant. Here is part of the conversation:

Naresh: So, you have this immense craving for the Death By Chocolate. What do you want instead?

Client: I want to have more control over my behavior.

Naresh: What does more control mean for you?

Client: It's like having a *Chapati*. I like it. But when I see it – I think whether I am hungry enough to have it? And also, I have it only as much as I want to. I don't keep eating it and I don't over stuff myself. But with DBC, I cannot seem to control my urge. If my pocket allows I can have it as much as my body can tolerate.

So, we elicited the Submodalities of the DBC and Chapati for her. We then made the Submodalities of DBC same as that of Chapati. This made her feel neutral about DBC. Also, when she went to the same chocolate parlor, she usually opted for different items to be able to enjoy variety.

This process is called mapping across Submodalities.

MAPPING ACROSS: GETTING RID OF FOOD CRAVINGS EXERCISE

Work with a partner if you have one. Designate one partner as A and the other as B. To begin with, B is the operator and A is the client.

Step One: Elicit the Submodalities of a food A loves and want to get rid of its craving

B to A: Imagine a food that isn't the healthiest choice, but that's one you crave for.

Using Table 1 B elicits the Submodalities of the food.

Step Two: Elicit the Submodalities of a food A is neutral about.

B to A: Now think of a food that you are neutral about.

B elicits the Submodalities of the food.

Step Three: The difference between the craved and neutral foods

There are some definite differences here, as there should be. One food you can't resist, and the other you are neutral about. The differences between the two are called *drivers*.

Analyze which Submodalities are drivers. Ignore the similarities.

Step Four: Mapping Across Submodalities

B to A: Now, again imagine the food you crave.

B guides A to change the driver Submodalities of the craved food to that of neutral food.

An example – if the image of the craved food is on the right side and closer to face, and that of the food you are neutral about is to left and far – make the image of the craved food to left and far. Make the size of picture of the craved food same as that of the food you are neutral about. Do this for as many Submodalities as possible.

Repeat this step few more time and at faster pace.

Step Five: Break state

Step Six: Test it

B to A: Now imagine the craved food again. How do you feel about it?

In this step A's response to the previously craved food should have changed to be similar to the food A is neutral about.

Switch roles.

TAKING CHARGE OF YOUR MOTIVATION

Think about something you don't feel motivated about but still you would like to do it. Maybe it's switching to a healthy diet, going to gym etc. Notice how the picture look – is it black or white? Is it small or big? Use the table 1 to elicit visual, auditory and kinesthetic Submodalities.

Now, think about something you are very much motivated about. Notice the pictures, sounds and feelings that you experience. Elicit the visual, auditory and kinesthetic Submodalties of this experience.

Let us call these experiences #1 (the one that you want to change) and #2 (which you already feel motivated about). Now, imagine both pictures in front of you. Next, make the Submodalities of the picture of experience #1 to that of experience #2. For example, if the color of the picture of the experience #1 (the one you want to change) is black and white, but the experience #2 (already motivated about) is colored – change the color of the picture of the experience #1 to that of experience #2. And so on. Do this to all the visual Submodalities. Then do the same to the auditory and kinesthetic Submodalities as well. Once you are done with all Submodalities, look around and move your body. Now think about the thing towards which you wanted to change your motivation levels. How do you feel about it now? If you have done this technique properly you will feel as motivated to do it now.

Here is step by step process. This can be done alone as explained above or with a partner.

TAKING CHARGE OF YOUR MOTIVATION EXERCISE

Work with a partner if you have one. Designate one partner as A and the other B.

Step One: Elicit the Submodalities of the activity that A is not motivated about but want to feel motivated about.

B to A: Imagine the activity that you aren't motivated about but want to feel motivated to do it.

B elicits the Submodalities of the activity using table 1.

Step Two: Elicit the Submodalities of something that A is motivated about.

B to A: Now, think of an activity that you are highly motivated about.

B elicits the Submodalities of the activity using table 1.

Step Three: Find the drivers

There are some definite differences between the thing that the client isn't feeling motivated about and the thing that he cannot resist. The differences between the two are called *drivers*.

Analyze which Submodalities are drivers. Ignore the similarities.

Step Four: Mapping Across Submodalities

B to A: Now, again think about the activity you aren't motivated about.

B guides A to change the driver Submodalities of the activity to those of the activity for which A is highly motivated about.

Repeat this step few times and at a faster pace.

Step Five: Break state

Step Six: Test it

B to A: Now, imagine the activity that you wanted to change your motivation levels about. How do you feel about it?

A should feel motivated about the activity.

Switch roles.

CHANGING LIMITING BELIEFS

Beliefs is a topic on which even books can be written. There are empowering beliefs which help you in your life to get things done. And then there are limiting beliefs which render you helpless. These are the biggest roadblocks in your success. Once those limiting beliefs are resolved, success seems more achievable and one can easily find the resources required to be successful.

Just like people, food, places you like or don't like, the beliefs are also given their meaning by the Submodalities. There are beliefs that you hold true and there are beliefs you don't hold true. Think about couple of beliefs you hold true – maybe the sun is going to arise tomorrow. You are going to do _______ tomorrow. Etc. Notice where the associated pictures come in your mind and their Submodalities. Now think about a belief that you don't think is true – e.g. the world is going to end tomorrow morning. Notice the Submodalities of the picture. Now, think of the belief that you held true once upon a time but you no longer believe – maybe belief in tooth fairy or Santa Claus. Notice where the picture shows up in your mind's eye and its Submodalities.

We can use the mapping across Submodalities technique to change a belief. There are many versions of this technique available. The below version is a simple one. The technique has two parts – making a belief untrue and replacing it with another belief. One thing you must keep in mind while working with belief is to be non-judgmental. No matter what belief the other person holds, it's service a purpose. And a belief should always be replaced with an equal or more powerful belief.

CHANGING LIMITING BELIEFS EXERCISE

Here is the process:

1. Think about a limiting belief that you have but wish you didn't have. Let us call it belief #1.
2. Is it okay to change this belief? Proceed if the answer is yes.
3. Elicit the visual, auditory and kinesthetic Submodalities associated with that belief.
4. Break state
5. Think about a belief that you once had but is no longer true. Let us call it belief #2.
6. Elicit the Submodalities of the belief that is no longer true.
7. Break state.
8. Find the differences in both beliefs.

9. Now, change the Submodalities of belief #1 to those of belief #2.

10. Break state.

11. Test – what do you think of _________________(insert belief #1). If the technique is done properly, belief #1 should sound no longer true.

12. Break state.

13. Think of a belief that is true for you, but without emotions. For example, the sun will rise tomorrow, it's _____ day tomorrow, etc. Let us call it #true-belief.

14. Elicit the Submodalities of this belief.

15. Break state.

16. Now, think of a positive belief that you would like to have instead. Let us call it #wished-belief.

17. Notice the pictures, sounds and feelings.

18. One by one map across the Submodalities of the #wished-belief to those of #true-belief.

19. Break state.

20. Test – Think about _______________(#wished-belief). How do you feel about it? If the technique is successful the #wished-belief belief should feel true.

21. Future pace: "Think of a time in the future when, if it had happened in the past, you would have believed ___________, and tell me what happens instead."

CHAPTER 5
MANAGING YOUR OWN STATE

You might have heard sentences like

"I wasn't in the right mental state when that happened"

"You need to be in flow to increase your productivity"

"Whenever I see her I feel anxious"

These are all examples of states.

WHAT IS A STATE IN NLP

A state in NLP refers to the sum total of the internal (mind) and external (physiological) states of a person at a particular moment of time.

The internal state refers to mental and emotional states.

Our state keeps changing as we move on in life. The results we get in an effort are determined by our state during the effort.

STATE MANAGEMENT

State management refers to consciously controlling one's state.

It's very important for us to be able to take charge of our state before it affects the quality of our lives.

Every great outcome including this book is nothing but outcome of continuous state management despite all the odds.

Champions are not the ones who always win races - champions are the ones who get out there and try. And try harder the next time. And even harder the next time. 'Champion' is a state of mind. They are devoted. They compete to best themselves as much if not more than they compete to best others. Champions are not just athletes. ~ Simon Sinek

TYPES OF STATES:

States can be categorized in following two ways:

1.   Resourceful and unresourceful states: Resourceful states are the states which help you achieve an outcome. For example, confidence, motivation are the resourceful states for achieving a professional goal. The unresourceful states are the ones which hinder you from achieving an outcome. For example – laziness is such a state. One thing to remember is that the state is in itself neither good or bad – the context makes it so. Laughter is a resourceful state generally – but is unresourceful when a person is attending a sad event. The other example is compassion – which is generally a resourceful state but not for the soldier fighting against a hardcore enemy. In NLP world you will use the terminology of resourceful and unresourceful (or not resourceful) states a lot.

2.   Uptime and Downtime states: These are two other states which you will come across a lot of times in NLP world especially with good NLP Trainers. An uptime state is an alert state – for example driving a vehicle in a new country for the first time or best when the vehicle is something that you have never driven before in your country. In this state your senses are tuned externally to the environment. Your visual, auditory and kinesthetic senses are in a high alert mode. You notice more while seeing, hearing and moving the steering. The feeling fades

away as you get used to the vehicle and roads. The opposite state is called a downtime state. This is a state when your senses are oriented internally. For example - in deep contemplation. Usually when you are contemplating something deeply – you cease to notice a lot of things happening around you. You kind of zone out. The other examples are a sleepy, drowsy state or a deep hypnotic trance.

Depending upon the context and technique you may need to put your clients in a particular resourceful or unresourceful state (for small time only). Also sometimes you may want them to be in a highly alert uptime state and other times you may want to induce a trance by putting them in a downtime state. In NLP Terms this is called eliciting a state. Let us learn more about state elicitation.

STATE ELICITATION

Do you recall someone who is an expert at irritating others? Or someone who's an expert at making people fall on the floor laughing?

These two are the best examples of the state elicitations.

State elicitation means getting someone into a particular state. We all do it with people all the time. For example, you may be an expert at frustrating some particular sort of people or you may be or have been the class clown, or the moment you enter the room the atmosphere might lighten up or you may be able to invoke respect in some people etc. One of the ways of state elicitation is to talk about an old incident. For example, discussing with someone about a tragedy that happened with them in the past or long cherished childhood memories. And during the discussion, most of the times the other person goes into the same state as they were in the past when that event happened.

State Elicitation in NLP is much of a conscious process. Here you can leverage the past events in their lives. For example, you can elicit a particular state, let's say of high motivation by asking the person to remember a time in the past when they felt motivated.

Below is the process for this.

STATE ELICITATION PROCESS

Below is the script for state elicitation. While practicing, do this only for the resourceful states like motivation, confidence, happiness etc.

Let's say that you want to elicit a state X (X= happiness/motivation etc.) in the client.

Tell the client:

- Think about a time when you felt *pure state* of **X**
- Relive the moment, as if it's happening now. See what you saw, hear what you heard and feel what you felt ... as if it's happening now. Feel the state of **X** building inside you.
- Increase the colors, increase the brightness and adjust the sounds or adjust them as you want to so as to intensify the state of X.
- If it's a picture, change it to a movie and if it's a movie, change it to a picture and notice if it intensifies the state. If the state is intensified then fine else reverse it to the old format.
- If it's 2D make it 3D and if it's 3D make it 2D and notice if it intensifies the state. If the state is intensified then fine else reverse to the old format.

STATE CALIBRATION

State calibration in simple words refers to being able to detect shift in state of a person.

In NLP, we hold a belief that mind and body are one. Whatever happens in your mind shows in your body and vice versa.

That means any shift in your mind will show up as a shift in your body also. For example, your body posture may shift as your mood changes or you associate into a past memory. If you're practicing this with a client and pay closer attention, then the person's facial muscle tone may shift or the face color may change. You may also notice the change in the pupil dilation or the size of the lower lip changing as a result of increase or decrease in blood flow.

One of the easiest clues is when the client takes a deep breath or has a swallow reflex.

Don't worry if you're unable to catch many or any of the above. You'll get a feeling most of the times that something has shifted in the other person.

Repeat the State Elicitation practice from previous section and calibrate the person before and after the activity.

IMPORTANT NOTES ABOUT STATE

The success or failure of a person in a project is function of the state management. Resourceful states enable us to achieve our goal faster. Unresourceful states hinder our progress in a particular goal and sometimes can stop our progress altogether.

New NLPers tend to generalize that the motivation, confidence etc. are resourceful states to have. However, they may not be resourceful when you're faced with an armed robber. The resourcefulness of a state is a function of its usefulness. The usefulness of a state should be evaluated in a context.

A particular state can be resourceful or not, depending upon the context. For example, an uptime state, which is a high alert state, is useful when you are driving but not when you are trying to meditate or sleep after a long day's work.

Hence, when a client asks that they need motivation and confidence, rather than jumping to anchoring the state you must ask – "When and where?"

BREAK STATE

Break state is a distraction which will break the flow of state. For example, you might be enjoying your favorite TV show or match and suddenly the phone rings and breaks your flow. While you move to pick up the phone, it changes your neurology by just the act of moving your awareness and body. This is an example of break state.

You might wonder whether break state is good or bad. And I would draw your attention to what we just discussed. It all depends upon the context. If you are doing something that needs immense focus, the break state will break your flow. In some instances, this may mean you have to redo the whole activity together. When I was very young, I used to go to my father's office. It was the time when there were no credit/debit cards and cash was the primary method of transaction. I remember several instances where my father would be counting a huge wad of currency notes and suddenly the phone would ring or some other distraction would happen. It would disrupt his flow. And after doing whatever was needful (answering the phone etc.), my father would seem to be lost in where he was with the counting. He would look at both his hands, try to recollect where the counting was and then many times start over again. The bigger the amount, the more will be the impact of distraction.

However, break states are useful when a state change can be useful. For example when a client is crying during a coaching session – an induced break state by you as a coach can help the client to come out of the crying cycle and give you an opportunity to shift their attention towards the solution to the problem.

You'll use a break state many times during the NLP techniques –for example, when you need to associate multiple states on a specific anchor (will be introduced later), you'll need to elicit multiple states in a short time. To avoid mixed states – it's better to use the break state after anchoring a state and before moving to the next one. The other use is to test the effectiveness of a technique. When you have just done a technique and test directly then the test almost always will be positive. It's like when you check the heart rate of a person after he has run a 100 meters – the rate will always be high. The right way is to allow the person to cool down before taking the reading. Break state is mental cooling down. Hence after doing a technique – do a break state – and then test whether the technique has worked.

HOW TO BREAK STATE

A break state is nothing but a distraction. You can achieve this in many ways, for example you may ask:

- Give me the last five digits of your mobile number.
- Give me the alternate digits of you mobile number.
- Give me the last five digits of your mobile number in reverse order.
- What is the color of the main door of your best friend's house.
- What did you have for breakfast?
- Any random conversation.
- Make it more innovative e.g. Do you smell a popcorn?
- You can have fun – Can you sing Twinkle Twinkle Little Star?

In our workshops we have a lot of fun with break states by using our mental creativity. Apart from encouraging people to use the creative hemisphere of their brains – these also serve as great ice breakers and loosen people.

CHAPTER 6
ANCHORING

Has it ever happened that the moment you look at someone's face you feel greatly elated or some other emotion. Sometimes you go to your hometown after a gap and as you are walking in the streets the aroma of a particular food sends you down to the memory lane to the joyful moments spent with family and friends. Both of these are examples of Anchors. An Anchor is a trigger which invokes some neurological response. In above two examples the sight of face and the smell of food are the examples of visual and gustatory triggers, which invoke past memories. The trigger can be visual, auditory, kinesthetic, olfactory and gustatory.

Anchors are always happening to you. As a living being you cannot avoid anchors. It's an unconscious process coming from your survival instinct. For example, our primitive ancestors had learned to automatically associate the face of sabretooth tiger with imminent danger. As soon as they would see that face, the conscious mind would stop and before they themselves knew they would be on their feet running for dear lives. You can imagine their plight if they had to analyze/calculate they risk every time they saw the face of the sabretooth tiger.

ANCHORING AS GENERALIZATION

The brain optimizes its functioning through the process of deletion, distortion and generalization. Anchoring is a form of generalization.

Every time a trigger happens (e.g. the smell of food, sight of a sabretooth tiger) the unconscious responds in a particular way.

Habits are sustained through Anchors.

ANCHORING IS UNCONSCIOUS

Anchoring is an unconscious process. As soon as the trigger happens the conscious mind stops working and unconscious takes over. "I know I shouldn't react like this in office but the moment I see his face I lose my control" – a client told me, whose ex happened to work in the same company. The client at conscious level knew that her reaction wasn't appropriate. People who fall in love associate the faces and the voices of the other person with particular neurological reaction. The conscious mind is out of question in such matters. Metaphorically we use the phrases that the person is blinded by love or love is blind etc.

TYPES OF ANCHORS

Anchors can be:

- Visual: Seeing an old movie poster reminds you of good old days.
- Auditory: The sound of an old car reminds you of the car that your father used to drive. Or someone talking in particular tone makes you feel in a certain way.
- Kinesthetic: You are making a bonfire. And as soon as you sit next to it, it makes you feel bit nostalgic and the memories of a big bonfire you made with your college group some years ago come rushing.
- Olfactory: The smell of freshly baked cake reminds you of your grandma's house.

- Gustatory: You are at a food festival. You taste something and it's exactly like the food your mother used to make. You feel as if you are 10-year-old child again.
- Complex: A combination of two or more of above mentioned types. For example, a person looking at you in a certain way (visual) and talking in a particular tone (auditory) reminds you of and old crush; and all you wish is the time to freeze for few moments or rewind to the old days.
- Spatial: These anchors are of special kind, which fall under complex anchors, but have space association. You will learn how to create Spatial Anchors in Circle of Excellence Technique.

ANCHORING PROCESS – BIRD'S EYE VIEW

Before we go forward, I want to give you a bird's eye view of the Anchoring process and few things you should take care of while Anchoring to make it effective. At the high level the anchoring in NLP has five steps:

1. State elicitation
2. Intensifying the state
3. Anchor the state
4. Break state
5. Test

GUIDELINES FOR EFFECTIVE ANCHORING

To make sure that you have good anchors which work, you need to follow certain guidelines.

1.   Purity of state: The state that you elicit should be a pure state. By pure state we mean that the state shouldn't be a mix of two or more states. E.g. you need to ask your client to think about a time when they felt a pure state of, let's say confidence. It shouldn't be confidence + motivation + happiness. Many times the state that the client want is going to be a combination of let's say Happiness, Confidence and Motivation. In that case elicit and Anchor these states one by one. This is called stacking the anchors. Never ask the client to remember a state when they felt happy, confident and motivated together.

2.   Intensity of state: The more intense the state the quicker and stronger is the anchor. You can intensify the state by asking the client to adjust the Submodalities of the state. For example, you can ask the client to increase the colors and brightness of the images they are seeing when accessing memories. Further they can make the images 3D and movie and check if it makes the difference. Similarly adjusting the volume can also intensify the state.

3.   Uniqueness of the Anchor: The Anchor that the client chooses should be unique. Most of the new NLPers/therapists think that it's a really cool idea to set a highly resourceful Anchor to something that the client does habitually or to something like shaking hands. However, this isn't a good idea. It's not going to be effective. Because they have done the same thing so many times habitually that there may already be number of states attached to that action. The Anchor should be unique like touching the back of hand, pulling left ear lobe etc.

4.   Timing of Anchor: The timing of Anchor is also very critical. When a state builds up, it will start from zero and gradually rise to peak. Subsequently it will start declining. You should set an Anchor when the state is near the peak on the rising side. Never set an Anchor

when the state is declining as at that time some other states may also get mixed up. In case the state starts declining before you begin installing the anchor – just break state and restart the process. If you cannot calibrate whether a states has built up, feel free to ask the client to signal you when their state is about to peak.

5.   Repetition of Anchor: An Anchor becomes stronger and stronger if it's reinforced repetitively. This means that setting same Anchor three times makes it stronger than setting it once. Ask the client to access a memory where they felt the state in purity. And Anchor the state when it peaks. Now ask the client to remember another memory where they felt the same state in purity. And Anchor this to the same anchor when it peaks. Do this 3-4 times and you will have a really strong Anchor.

ANCHORING PROCESS IN DETAIL

With this, we're ready for the process of setting the Anchor. In the below example, we will learn how to anchor a state of motivation to touch on knuckles. I like knuckles because they are static. They don't move and they are easier to calibrate.

1.   Elicit state: Before the first step go into the state yourself. Using a motivated body language and voice tone ask the person to think about a time in past when he felt a pure state of motivation.

2.   Intensify the state: Ask the client to make the image bigger, brighter, more colorful and become fully associated in the memory. Make it 3D and panoramic and add more details.

3.   Anchor: As you do above steps, keep calibrating the person for signs of accessing a motivated state e.g. change in

breathing, change in skin color, change in voice tone if the client is speaking (some clients do talk as they access new states), change in tightness in body etc. And when you notice these changes just touch the client on one of his knuckles for few seconds. After some time you may notice the state shifting again. Remove the anchor at this time.

4. Break state. Ask the client to give you the last five digits of his mobile number, or the color of his first car etc. You can have fun with starting an interesting conversation at this step.

5. Test. Fire the anchor and notice whether the physiology of the client shifts to the one that you noticed upon state elicitation in step 1. If you cannot make out, just ask the client how he/she feels.

NEGATIVE ANCHORS

Anchoring is an unconscious process. The highest priority task of the unconscious mind is the physical survival. In the process of fulfilling this task the unconscious mind many times unnecessarily overgeneralizes and associates some triggers with non-resourceful states. For example, you may dislike someone so much that after a while just the mention of person's name may put you into a bad state. This is a negative anchor. Suppose you have to work with that person and you need complete co-operation with that person. Now you will not only be hearing the person's name but also interacting with the person over a period of time.

And sometimes you may not be even aware of the source of anchor and yet suffering. For example, I have seen some cases in India where the clients described feeling gloomy in particular weather especially in the evenings. Upon further investigation we found that they started feeling so after the college. And more questions lead to the conclusion that the anchor was formed when the person was in the final year and they were going to be separated from their classmates with whom they had developed a strong bond over 3-4 years. Even highly insensitive students feel sad in those days. In the evenings after the college the groups would gather and discuss the time spent together and usually people would feel sad that such time won't come again after that summer. This associated that particular weather with sadness. The next time (which may happen even after several years) the same weather would trigger the feelings stored in the subconscious mind in the final year to surface and the person would feel sad.

The negative anchors result into non-resourceful states and may hamper the productivity. Sometimes the reaction to these triggers is so severe that the person is unable to think or act straight.

Such anchors should be collapsed.

COLLAPSING ANCHORS

Just as there are techniques in NLP to set resourceful anchors – there are techniques to dissolve or collapse non-resourceful anchors. The basic principle behind collapsing is very simple. Suppose you have a glass of hot milk – what is the quickest way to cool it? The answer is to keep adding cold milk to it until the desired temperature is reached.

In collapsing negative anchors also you need to use the same principle – i.e. use a positive anchor to nullify the effects of the negative anchors.

Here is the technique:

1. Anchor the negative state (Anchor A) to say the left hand of the client. Say the client feel sad in a situation.
2. Break state.
3. Anchor an opposite positive state, i.e. happiness in this case (Anchor B), to the right hand of the client. Stack the anchor 2-3 times to make sure the anchor is very powerful.
4. Break state.
5. Fire Anchor B for few seconds – let the state build up and then fire Anchor A – hold for few seconds and then release anchor A and keep Anchor B there.
6. Break state and repeat steps 5 and 6 three to five times.
7. Break state.
8. Test – Fire Anchor A – the negative state shouldn't be triggered. Ask the client to think about what would trigger sadness and ask him to think about the trigger and try to get into the non-resourceful state. The client shouldn't be able to enter into the negative state.

CHAPTER 7
CONNECTING TO PEOPLE – BUILDING RAPPORT

To get anything done from someone the first requirement is to be able to connect to them at appropriate level and then lead them to what you want them to do.

There are multiple levels of connection ranging from wishy washy connection to a deep level connection of oneness.

The desired level of connection will vary depending upon the context. For example, in the context of a marriage you will want a physical, emotional and probably a spiritual level connection. However, in professional context you may want a connection of trust, openness, respect, commitment and professionalism. A physical level connection in the reporting chain, will be highly inappropriate. Similarly, a Spiritual level connection is also not required in this context. While connecting to friends, you should have a connection of trust, respect, fun and intimacy. Professionalism won't be appropriate aspect of this connection. How will you feel if you are meeting a longtime friend and that person turns up into a business suit and tries to sell insurance to you. On the other hand, consider that the same friend shows up in business suit but as soon as he sees you, he comes running and hugs you tightly like he used to do in school time and starts speaking in the same slang as he used to. Won't you feel that your friend has not changed a bit?

RAPPORT

The level of connection we have with someone is called Rapport. You need appropriate level of rapport depending upon context.

Rapport is a sense of connection characterized by appropriate level of openness and responsiveness.

You cannot see it. You cannot hear it. You can only sense the level of connection. Inside your body you will feel it in some part of your body. For example, in heart area and/or abdomen. Some people feel it in their head. It's different for different people.

HOW TO DEVELOP RAPPORT

There are many techniques for developing rapport at any level.

Matching/Mirroring Body Language

In matching/mirroring technique you can match or mirror a person's body language behavior at multiple levels.

You sit in the same posture as the person is sitting. If they're sitting cross legged you sit cross legged. If they have their arms folded, you fold your arms as well.

If during conversation they change their posture. You also change your posture with a time lag of say 20-30 seconds.

The difference between matching and mirroring is that in matching you will match them exactly. If their right leg is above left, you will also keep your right leg above left.

In mirroring, you act as a mirror. Hence, if they have their right leg above left leg, you sit with your left leg above right i.e. in mirror position.

In this technique care should be taken not to match exactly. Otherwise, the person may feel that you are mimicking them.

Also, don't match the whole behavior to avoid detection. Hence, if they're raising their hand from leg to the back of their head, you just raise your hand from leg to the level of chest and put it down. This will send them subtle signal that you're in rapport with them.

Giving The Keywords Back

At this level, you match their key phrases. Here is a conversation:

Ryan: Hi.. I am Ryan from India.

Michelle: Hi… I am Michelle from UK.

Ryan: Nice to meet you, Michelle. What do you do?

Michelle: Same here. I am a trainer.

Ryan: Ah… a trainer, what kind of trainer?

Michelle: I am a soft skills trainer. I train people in developing influencing skills.

Ryan: Okies… you are a soft skills trainer who trains people in influencing skills… This is new to me.. could you please elaborate what do you mean by influencing skills….

And the conversation goes on. In all lines Ryan is repeating some keywords of key phrases back to Michelle.

Matching The Representational Mode

When you're talking to someone, listen to the verbal predicates they are using. Pace the representational mode. For example, if the other person is using visual words, then use visual words. And if at some point the person switches to kinesthetic, then switch to kinesthetic words.

Assume The Rapport Is There

This is the fastest way of developing rapport. In this technique, you assume and act as if the rapport is already there. The minds of both parties will catch up very fast to fulfill the gap.

Matching The Auditory Behavior

You calibrate how the person is speaking and match their auditory qualities.

- Voice tonality
- Volume Levels
- Pitch
- Rhythm
- Rate/Speed of speaking

How To Test Rapport?

The techniques of matching/mirroring are called pacing. That is, you are pacing the experience of the other person.

You can test the rapport by leading the other person.

When you want to test rapport, just slightly shift your posture or do some hand movement etc. If the other person follows you unconsciously, then this indicates rapport.

The purpose of rapport in all cases, for example - selling or change work, is leading the person. Even when you're building rapport for better relationship, you are leading the other person into a space of mutual trust, respect and harmony.

Final Words On Rapport

In most of NLP Trainings a lot of emphasis is given to Rapport building. This is however blowing this out of proportion.

You don't need deepest levels or rapport with each and every one. You just need enough rapport so that the other person trusts you and is open to talking to you on the subject.

Also, you don't need to come in rapport with each and every one. For example, it doesn't make any sense of coming in rapport with someone who intends to harm others.

There is a wrong assumption that it takes a long time to build rapport. For example, in one training participants were told to match or mirror someone for 20-30 minutes. This isn't practical. No one will give a tele-caller 20-30 minute to develop rapport before coming to the point. You don't need extraordinary levels of rapport with everyone. You just need sufficient rapport to be able to lead the person.

CHAPTER 8
DISSOLVING MENTAL BLOCKS

All of us have certain mental blocks that stop from reaching our goals or at least slow us down. This is like driving the car with handbrakes on.

What is the logical thing to do in such case? Some people would push the accelerator harder and harder. This will help temporarily but will also damage the car and you'll still be slow.

However, the easier and effortless way is just to release the hand brake.

In this chapter we are going to go through some of the techniques that help in dealing with the mental blocks. As you'll notice – these techniques are fast, effective and painless. The most wonderful thing about these is that they're content free.

WHAT ARE MENTAL BLOCKS?

The mental blocks are things you carry in your mind that stop you from reaching your peak potential in any context. For example, fear of heights, phobias of closed spaces, memories of the events that happened long time ago but still powerful enough to not let you focus on your goal, non-resourceful behaviors etc.

WHERE DO THE MENTAL BLOCKS COME FROM?

You acquire the mental blocks unconsciously as a part of living on this earth.

When you were born – you were born without any mental blocks except two – the fear of loud noises and fear of falling. The reason that nature equipped you with these fears was to ensure you're aware of potential dangers. Whenever these fears got triggered e.g. the whistle of pressure cooker or a loud horn – your nervous system automatically interpreted it as a potential danger, and you responded by crying out loudly for the help until some adult came down and consoled you – that was your way to make sure that all was well.

Do you realize how useful these fears were for you? In NLP we have presupposition - every behavior has got an underlying positive intention. These fears were useful for your survival.

All other mental blocks are acquired after birth. And the above presupposition is true for the other mental blocks as well.

Almost in all cases, the main intention of your mental blocks is to protect you from some harm. For example, the fear of burning is a mental block which keeps you away from fire. Similarly, the fear of public speaking also is a mental block so as to save you from emotional pain of feeling embarrassed.

These mental blocks are acquired through the intentional (a grown up making you aware of how dangerous _____ is) or accidental programming (learned through own negative experiences) – most of which happens during our childhood. It's said that we learn most of our lessons in the first seven years and from there onwards we keep reliving those lessons for the rest of our lives. This doesn't mean that we don't acquire mental blocks after seven years of age. The human brain never stops learning. Acquiring mental blocks is possible even at the last breath – as many past life regressionists would testify.

Coming back to the childhood - the mental programming of a child happens in two ways.

First way is through the environment i.e. parents, teachers, siblings, friends etc. Apart from this there is programming by media like Television, mobile phones, tablets etc.

We can call it SEER conditioning. SEER conditioning stands for Social, Economic, Education and Religious conditioning. The subconscious mind of the child is very impressionable. The children in first seven years are in a hypnotic state – where they are highly suggestible. Your mind at this stage is like a clean slate. Anything can be written on it by anyone. Your mind hasn't yet developed the conscious filter during this period. So, whatever is repeatedly bombarded onto your head - gets accepted and made part of the mental programming.

The second way in which you learn during childhood is through your own experiences. For example, at this stage, you may playfully touch a hot cup of tea/coffee. This would result in pain. And henceforth you would always be careful about touching the hot cup again.

At this stage you may go to the stage to speak something in a function and accidentally fumble or forget your lines. This may be followed by hooting by classmates. Your subconscious mind then may associate the public speaking with possible embarrassment. With every repeat incident (real or imaginary), it would strengthen this program – leading to developing lifelong stage fear.

IS THE CHANGE DIFFICULT?

Now, the next question which might come to your mind is - is it possible to deal with the mental blocks? If yes, how easy or difficult is it to do so?

And the answer is contained in the NLP Presupposition – Human beings are capable of one-trial learning.

If phobia can be acquired in one incident, then it can be unlearned in one go also. Once you have sufficient understanding of how the brain and mind work, it'll be very easy for you to work with anyone and help them get rid of the fear/phobias and bad memories. For this, I would invite you to revisit the basics of NLP like NLP Sub-modalities, NLP Communication model etc.

The following sections contain the techniques for releasing these mental blocks.

GETTING RID OF BAD MEMORIES

Getting rid of bad memories is very easy using NLP. A bad memory is nothing but a memory with a negative emotional charge attached to it.

Depending upon person, the same memory can be a learning experience or a bad memory. For example, two persons might get into a relationship with each other and eventually break up. Of course, it has affected both of them. However, one of them would take it as a learning experience for the future relationships, while the other may get stuck in life due to the horrible breakup. This memory will keep replaying the second person's mind over and over, building more and more resentment which ultimately may result in diseases or total refrain from entering into new relationships or a pattern of failed relationships. In other words the result of getting stuck in bad memory is bad most of the times.

On the other hand, the other person might mourn the event for some time, then consolidate the learnings and get into new relationship. And because of the learnings from previous relationship, this person won't repeat the same mistake and lead a healthier relationship.

The event is same. However, both persons have attached two different meanings to it and that has determined their future lives.

Hence, a bad memory is nothing but the meaning and thus the emotional charge we associate with it. Once we remove the emotional charge, take all the learnings from event, we get unstuck in life and it becomes easier to move on.

ELEVATOR TECHNIQUE - TURN BAD MEMORIES INTO LEARNING EXPERIENCES

Elevator technique is a simple and easy NLP technique. However, it'll be a big mistake to associate the simplicity of this technique with its effectiveness. So far, this technique has served me and my clients very well. Except for one case, where I was working with an elderly person, this technique has 100% success rate.

The beauty of this technique is that it involves taking the lesson from the event. And once the lesson is taken from the event, the possibility of event repeating again in life i.e. settling into pattern is reduced drastically. Also, if there's already a pattern, the pattern has more likelihood of getting broken if the learning from the experience is complete.

Here is the technique:

1.   [To the client] Think about the event or memory which is bad memory for you. Relive this event as if it's happening now. See what you saw, hear the sounds that you heard and feel the feelings that this memory invokes in you. I will ask you certain questions about the pictures and sounds, without getting into the details just answer in one or two words:

a.   How are the images – are they big or small?

b.   How are the sounds – are they loud or soft?

c.   How do you feel? Just name the feeling in one word.

2.   Now imagine that there is a staircase behind you. Mentally leave yourself there and take the staircase and go one floor above. From the one floor above, look at the event one floor below.

a.   How are the images – are they big or small?

b.   How are the sounds – are they loud or soft?

c.   How do you feel? *[The feelings would be there but reduced]*.

3.   Now, imagine that there's an elevator behind you. This is world's tallest elevator. Go inside the elevator and go five floors above. (*Wait for 2-3 seconds, don't give much time here*). Now come out the elevator and look down at the event was happening below.

a.   How are the images – are they big or small? (*the higher the client goes the smaller the images will become*)

b.   How are the sounds – are they loud or soft? (*The higher the client goes the softer the sounds will become and ultimately the client won't be able to hear anything*)

c.   How do you feel? *(With picture and sounds changing the feeling will keep reducing as the levels increase)*

d.   *If the feelings are gone then go to the next step. Else go to the beginning of step 3 and take the client to the higher levels.*

4.   Break state. Ask some random questions to distract the client.

5.   Test. Ask the client to think about the event again. They won't be able to access the old feelings.

The elevator technique is also known as the progressive dissociation technique. This is based upon the fact that the brain stores the memories in certain format i.e. with certain set of Sub-modalities. Any change in these Sub-modalities will result in corresponding change in the feelings.

In progressive-dissociation we first dissociate the client and with time keep dissociating him further and further. This also results in changing in the size of the images and decrease of the volume of the sounds leading. With every level, the intensity of the feelings keep reducing and after a particular level the feelings will become neutral.

GETTING RID OF FEARS/PHOBIAS

One of the uses of NLP is to get rid of fears and phobias. Most of people are confused between what is a fear or phobia. Hence, it's essential to clarify what is fear and what is phobia.

FEARS VS PHOBIAS

Most of the people are confused between fears and phobias. The confusion is so wide that when someone describes their phobia to you, the chances are that they are talking about their fear. And their fear could be so intense that they easily confuse it with phobia.

The difference is that the phobia is the fear of fear. For example, a person with the height phobia, is not only afraid of heights, but the mere thought of going up and being afraid to death creates another fear i.e. the fear of being afraid to death.

As a result, the reaction to phobia is instantaneous for a person.

An example could be a person having fear of snakes can talk about his fear without feeling anything. However as soon as he sees the actual snake or even if someone just mentions that there is a snake under his chair, he may jump 6 feet high in the air.

However, a person with snake phobia cannot even talk about snakes without freaking out.

FAST PHOBIA CURE TECHNIQUE

Fast Phobia Cure is an NLP technique, which can be justifiably called the poster boy of NLP. Thousands of NLP courses sell just because of this technique. And it's integral to any NLP course.

One thing to be noted is that though the name of this technique is the phobia cure, it can be used for anxieties due to future events or bad memories etc.

Fast Phobia Cure #1

o   Mentally create a 2-3 minute movie of the phobia or event you want to work on. The movie will start from point A, when things are going fine and then the phobia or the event happens, end at point B when the things are normal again.

1.   Imagine that you are sitting in the middle row of a movie theater. In front of you there is the screen. And behind you and above, there is the projector room.

2.   Your mental movie is going to play on this screen. So just bring in the first screen of the movie and freeze it on the screen.

3.   As you do this, leave your body there on the middle row and float above and behind to the projection booth, so that now you can see yourself sitting in the middle row and seeing the first scene of the movie frozen on the screen.

4.   Now turn the scene black and white and quickly run the movie forward in couple of seconds in black and white and freeze it at the last scene.

5.   Now float out of the projection booth and float inside your body in the middle row. Notice how it feels.

6.   Now float out of your body in the middle row and float to the screen and get associated in the last scene of the movie.

7.   Now, turn the picture into colored one and run the movie backwards very fast in few seconds and freeze the screen at the first scene.

8.   Again float out of the screen and float back into your body in the middle seat and turn the picture into a black and white one.

9.   Repeat steps 1-8 for three to four times.

o   Break state: Move your body. Mentally recite the last five digits of you mobile number in reverse etc.

o   Test: Try to access the fear/phobia or the bad memory and try to feel bad. And notice that your response to the phobia stimuli or the event has changed now. Most of people aren't even able to get themselves feel bad. And many of the people working on bad memories are unable to access the memory at this point.

Fast Phobia Cure #2

This is far simpler process than the first process and takes lesser time. It's also easier to remember.

o   Mentally create a 2-3 minute movie of the phobia or event you want to work on. The movie will start from point A, when things are going fine and then the phobia or the event happens, end at point B when the things are normal again.

1.   Imagine that you are sitting in the middle row of a movie theater. In front of you there is the screen. And behind you and above, there is the projector room.

2.   Your mental movie is going to play on this screen. So just bring in the first screen of the movie and freeze it on the screen.

3.   As you do this, leave your body there on the middle row and float above and behind to the projection booth, so that now you can see yourself sitting in the middle row and seeing the first scene of the movie frozen on the screen.

4.   Now turn the scene black and white and quickly run the movie forward in couple of seconds in black and white and freeze it at the last scene.

5.	Now run this movie backwards in black and white for 5-6 times very very fast so that it doesn't take more than 3-5 seconds to run whole movie.

o	And every time you reverse you distort the movie little bit. You can change the voices to the Donald duck's voice, put Donald duck faces all over etc.

6.	Mentally create a 2-3 minute movie of the phobia or event you want to work on. The movie will start from point A, when things are going fine and then the phobia or the event happens and, end at point B

o	Break state: Move your body. Mentally recite the last five digits of your mobile number in reverse etc.

o	Test: Try to access the fear/phobia or the bad memory and try to feel bad. And notice that your response to the phobia stimuli or the event has changed now. Most of the people aren't even able to get themselves feel bad. And many of the people working on bad memories are unable to access the memory at this point.

The Fast Phobia cures is based upon the NLP concept called double dissociation. As the name implies in double dissociation we dissociate the client twice. The first level is when the client is sitting in the chair in the cinema hall and the movie of the experience is on the screen. The second level of dissociation comes into picture when we tell the client to leave his body in the seat and float into the projection booth. Thus, the client can see his movie on the screen and his body sitting in the middle chair watching the movie and he himself having the feeling of being in the projection booth.

The double dissociation is much more powerful and far more effective technique than single level of dissociation.

Apart from fear and phobias, this technique can also be used for bad memories, anxiety or handling any other situation causing stress or other negative emotions.

It so happens that after the technique most of the clients are unable to access the fear or phobic reaction. If you're working with a bad memory case, then after the technique the person may have complete amnesia of the event itself.

CHAPTER 9
HANDLING CONFLICTS

Whether we like them or not, the conflicts are part of our lives. A person who says he doesn't have any conflict is a liar. The conflicts arise at two levels.

The first type is the external conflict where you're in a conflict with someone else. This type of conflicts strain relationships and productivity especially if you have to work with the person. Sometimes the person is very important to you. In such case even if you don't have to work together your mind keeps wandering into negativity and doesn't let you focus on the tasks at hand. You might be able to relate to such heart-burns from past. You can think of the romantic relationships, or relationships between an employee and his manager, relationships with business partners or with important customers etc. The ongoing conflicts in these relationships can jeopardize the relationship permanently and significantly affect your life.

The second type of the conflict is internal conflict. This happens when you seem to be split into two parts and both parts seem to be on war. I had a friend. He was addicted to chocolate. Almost every day after having half kilogram of chocolate he would pledge not to have the chocolate again, and the next day again he would be at the chocolate café. One part of his mind wanted to enjoy the chocolate and the other part wanted him to lead a free and healthy life. Similarly, the conflict between two parts in deciding to go to a gym versus watching favorite show on television at home is an example of internal conflict. As you can see - the internal conflicts are part of our day to day lives.

The internal conflicts can also result in delaying of important decisions like getting married or not, getting a job or starting a business etc.

We're better off resolving the internal or external conflicts as soon as possible. Prolonged conflicts of any kind result in stress and can jeopardize the life of the person going through these conflicts and also lives of people around him.

NLP gives you techniques to easily and effortlessly resolve both kinds of conflicts.

MANAGING EXTERNAL CONFLICTS

Man is a social animal. This comes from the primitive days, when living in herds was used by most of mammals to stay warm and to feel safe from predators.

Till now, we survive and thrive along other human beings. It has been proven that teamwork brings in better results than the sum total of the productivities of the individuals in the team. That is if there are seven members in the team then the productivity of the team is higher than 7x. It's not 7x.

For example, a husband wife couple is a team which runs house, raises children etc. This team can raise two children in much more effortlessly than if each of them had raise one child with complete responsibility. That is the team power isn't 2x, but much more than 2x.

The historical Taj Mahal or Pyramids, all great monuments which baffle even the modern generation of scientists were built through team work.

We need other people to not only work and produce results but to share our stories, have the sense of accomplishment, external validation etc. Research has proven that people who have better social connections, tend to live a greater number of years.

Hence, it's important to have healthy connections with people in your lives. The main reason for conflict is difference in perceptions. In NLP terms, every person has their own personal map of the world. Everyone has different ways of looking at the problems as well as solutions. That is there's always a difference of opinion between any two persons. Even if two persons agree on the same thing, the extent to which they agree differs.

Many times, this difference in opinions leads to the inter-personal conflicts. And if these conflicts aren't handled in mature way, they not only damage the relationships but the purpose of each of those relationships. For example, a conflict in husband and wife, doesn't only damage the relationship between the couple but also affects the way the house is run and the ideal upbringing of the children.

As I mentioned, the inter-personal conflicts are natural to occur due to differences in personal maps. NLP provides an excellent way to handle these conflicts.

PERCEPTUAL POSITIONS TECHNIQUE FOR EXTERNAL CONFLICTS

Perceptual positions is NLP technique to handle external conflicts. If you've heard the saying that one should put himself in others' shoes to understand their side of the story – then that is essentially what we do in this technique.

For doing this exercise, you need sufficient space where there are four points where you can easily sit or stand. For example, a room with less furniture where you can stand in four corners. Or four tiles on a floor. Or four chairs etc.

These all work fine. My favorite is having two chairs to sit and two points to stand.

Here is how the setup looks like:

Chair 1 and chair 2 are kept facing each other.

Chair 1 represents your position. This is called first perceptual position.

Chair 2 represents the person with whom you have the conflict. This is called second perceptual position.

The position 3, represents neutral "fly on wall" position. In NLP we call it third perceptual position. I have found it works better if it's far from chair 1 and 2, in such a way that it doesn't interfere in the dynamics between first and second perceptual position. It can see and hear both positions, but it cannot give advice or talk to any of them, it can just observe. This position is also called fly on the wall position. It can be standing or sitting position. I prefer to have it standing position.

Point 4 is farther away from all three positions. This is anchor to fourth perceptual position. In NLP world we call it meta-position. Meta-position means a position above positions. I call it Buddha position to capture the gist of this position. It can see and hear all three positions. However, it's a timeless and boundless position – much like enlightened Buddha.

Also, like most of NLP processes it is a content free process. You need to not ask the details about what a person is going through at each step. I prefer to have the person do it silently even when I'm guiding. I tell them to nod their head when they're done with a step.

Here is the script of the process:

• Think about one external conflict that you're going through. Give me a nod once you are done. (wait for the nod)

• Now go to the first chair. This is the first perceptual position. This is your position in the conflict. Sit down in the chair and mentally go through what your thoughts are, and how do you feel about this whole situation. How do you react as a result of these feelings? And how is this impacting your life and relationship(s)? Take your time to process without saying any word. Give me a nod once you are done. (wait for the nod)

• Now, leave your mental image in the first chair and physically go to the second chair. This is the second perceptual position. This is the position of the other party in the conflict. Sit down in the chair and take the body language of the other person. Now, act as if you're the other person. Mentally go through what this persons' thoughts are, and how does he/she feel about this whole situation. How does this person react as a result of these feelings? And how is this impacting this person's life and relationship(s)? Take your time to process without saying any word. Give me a nod once you are done. (wait for the nod)

• Now leave this person in the chair and go to the third position. This is the position of the neutral observer. Stand in this position. This person isn't attached to any of the first or second positions. He/she is non-judgmental about the conflict. Mentally go through what does this neutral observer think and feel about the whole conflict between two persons. Give me a nod once you are done. (wait for the nod)

• Leave this position also and now go to the fourth position. This is meta-position or Buddha position. Be in this position and think about what does this evolved being think about this conflict. What does he think about the significance of this conflict across time, dimension, space and reality. Mentally process all that and give me a nod once you are done. (wait for the nod)

• Now, take all the learnings from this position and silently go to the first position. Sit in the chair and silently integrate all the learnings. Give me a nod once you are done. (wait for the nod).

• Break state

• How do you feel about this conflict?

In the last step when you ask the client how does he feel about the conflict, you will usually notice a change of voice and clarity of thoughts. The person would invariably describe that the conflict is insignificant or something better.

This is a powerful exercise which I do in almost all of my team or relationship coaching sessions. You can use and integrate this in your therapy, counseling, coaching or consulting where the person is dealing with some external conflict. It's better for them to develop their insights. The insights developed from inside are much more powerful than the same insights coming from a therapist, counselor, coach or the consultant.

The best part is that since it's content free, you are also saved from needless details of the conflict, and the client's efforts to justify his position which may otherwise require your intervention. Being content free also makes it very fast. And since the solution is coming from the client – the client is going to assume 100% responsibility to honor it.

It's important to be able to switch between perceptual positions to have a greater perspective about a situation. It has been observed that some people get stuck in a particular perceptual position. The people who are always stuck in the first perceptual position, become egocentric – always thinking about themselves and what is in a situation for them. They are least bothered about the needs and emotions of the others. On the other hand, some people are always stuck into second position. They are always putting others needs before themselves. These people are very sensitive to others' needs. This leads to ignoring their own health and well-being. And then, there are people who are always associated into the third position. These people tend to be dissociated from the world and are neutral to things happening around them.

MANAGING INTERNAL CONFLICTS

Similar to interpersonal conflicts one can have intra-personal or internal conflicts. And internal conflict is when one part of your mind wants to do something and the other part wants to avoid it or do something else.

For example, one part of your mind may want to go to the gym while the other part wants to avoid the pain. One part may want to have a chocolate bar while other part wants to lose weight. One part, may want to start his own business while the other part wants to stay in 9-5 job and not take risks.

Internal conflicts are paralyzing. They destroy the clarity in life and create confusion and inaction. Even if there is action, it's half-hearted and doesn't bear the same kind of results as the actions coming from the congruency.

Metaphorically, the internal conflict is as if your unconscious mind has split into two persons having different personalities. And both are in conflict with each other. This conflict often brings things to a standstill.

If two wrestlers are fighting with each other, they end up damaging each other. And when the wrestlers are fighting with each other, they may also do damage to the ground where they are fighting on. The same is true for the parts of the mind fighting each other. They wither each other out and also damage their fighting ground - your body. As a result, you may feel lack of willingness or lack of energy to act, lack of clarity etc. A prolonged internal conflict often results in diseases in the body.

It's therefore of utmost importance to resolve the internal conflicts and restore the congruency. It helps you to be in high energy levels, have clarity of thoughts, actions with purpose and mastery over whatever you do.

In NLP, we have a technique called visual squash to handle such conflicts.

VISUAL SQUASH TECHNIQUE FOR INTERNAL CONFLICTS

Visual Squash technique for managing internal conflicts is based upon the fact that the mind and all parts of the mind are there to serve you. They're there to fulfill some positive intention for you. Even if two parts are in conflict – both parts have some positive intention for you. At the surface level the positive intentions may not be visible. A little deeper contemplation may reveal these positive intentions to avoiding pain or having pleasure. At the deepest level all parts of the mind are working towards helping you survive.

Here is the technique. Work with a partner. Designated A and B among yourselves. Let A start the process with B as client.

1.   Think of an internal conflict that you want to deal with.

2.   Spread both your hands in front of you, palms facing upwards.

3.   Project the part which is stopping you from doing something on one of your hands. Create a mental image of this part in the form of a person. How does this part look, sound and feels like? Make it as real as much you can.

4.   Project the other part on the other hand. Create a mental image of this part in the form of a person. How does this part look, sound and feels like? Make it as real as much you can.

5.   Now look at the first part and ask it – What is its positive intention for you? Note the positive intention down.

6.   Look at the second part and ask it - What is its positive intention for you? Make a note of the answer.

7.   Do following steps in a loop until you find a common positive intention for both parts (e.g. both parts want to make the client happy)

a.   Now look at the first part again and ask – what is its positive intention behind <its previous answer> (For example if the positive intention in previous answer was to "be comfortable", your question should be – what is its positive intention behind helping you be comfortable)

b.   Now look at the first part again and ask – what is its positive intention behind its previous answer> (For example if the positive intention in the previous answer was to "be comfortable", your question should be – what is its positive intention behind helping you be comfortable)

c.   Repeat until you find a common positive intention

Example: You may end up hierarchy for each part like:

Part A: Comfort -> Avoid Pain -> happiness -> love

Part B: Avoid conflict -> Motivation -> energy -> happiness

(In this example both parts have 'happiness' as common positive intention. The part A said happiness in the third level, and part B said it in the fourth iteration. Hence, the intention can match at different hierarchy levels for both parts. It's fine as long as we have at least one common positive intention. As a coach, you should let go of the need for perfection. In the realm of mind things are seldom perfect or static. The next time you do this exercise you may get same answers at different levels. As long as both parts are able to come up with same positive intentions it doesn't matter at which level they are matching.)

8. Realize that both parts actually have many positive intentions for you. They are serving you.

9. Also, realize that both parts have ultimately the same positive intention <name of common positive intention> for you.

10. Make both parts face each other. And have them negotiate with each other about how can they help each other fulfill this common positive intention. What does each part expect from the other and how each part can serve other's expectations? Make this negotiation look, sound and feel real. Again, this conversation is seldom going to be perfect. Both parts may have to give something up in order to get something of greater value. Take your time until both parts are satisfied.

11. Now, bring your hands closer and make them touch each other with palms still facing upwards. Allow both parts to merge into a new being having the positive characteristics of bother parts. Now, bring your hands closer to your chest and press the hands against your chest and allow your mind to integrate the energy of resulting part.

12. Break state

13. Think about the conflict again. (The conflict should have vanished by now)

14. Switch roles

CHAPTER 10
GOAL SETTING: DECIDING WHAT DO YOU WANT

Cat: Where are you going?

Alice: Which way should I go?

Cat: That depends upon where you are going.

Alice: I don't know.

Cat: Then it doesn't matter which way you go.

-Lewis Caroll, Alice in Wonderland

We all have dreams – about our lives, our future, our relationships, career, finances, etc. Dreams are what give direction to life. However, most of the times, the dreams never materialize. People continue dreaming and yet live average or sub-average lives. For them – an enriched life is always a dream to be filled at some point of time in the future. The dreams are like castles in the air. They don't have foundation. This stops or delays their realization.

There are several things required to turn dream into reality.

First step to realize a dream is setting goal(s) to realize that dream. A goal is a dream with legs. We're always fulfilling goals – and most of the time they are others' goals. Others mean corporations, parents, friends, children etc. If you don't set goals for yourself, someone else will set them for you. So you end up living your life on someone else's terms. You work towards reaching targets from corporations, you plan your marriage and kids due to social pressure, you get into many activities due to peer pressure etc. While we cannot rule out any external interference for anyone and more or less everyone will do something or other due to external pressure – you will be able to live your life more on your terms when you have your priorities defined and when those priorities supported by goals. A person whose priority is to spend more time with his family will choose the career and corporation which will meet this demand. His financial goals may not be sky high. Even though we would like to have it all – there are tradeoffs. There is no career where you can spend less time and earn like Bill Gates.

"What is a goal?", you may ask. As you know, dreams are things you aspire to achieve. They keep floating around. You dream one thing today and the dream changes after few days. The dreams just stick around or fade away. They stick around because they don't have legs which will move them around. They fade because they grow dull when no action is taken to achieve them. A goal is a dream with legs. Goal gives grounding or foundation to the dreams. The bigger the dreams the more important is goal setting. This is the reason that most of successful corporates spend a lot of time in goal setting. Goals are set from the corporate level, to department level, to team and till the individual employees. This is how corporates with few dozens to millions of employees are run. Hence, if you're working for a corporate, you are already working towards some goals – regardless of whether you like goal setting or not.

A goal is a statement of desired result that you want to achieve. The desired result can be to be better off financially or materialized a dream relationship etc. It can also be to get into great physical shape or to contribute more meaningfully to a cause you believe in and so on.

Earlier, goal setting was limited mainly to corporates. With time people realized the effectiveness of goal setting process and started using it for their career and eventually personal life goals as well. Today even the students set goals to beat the competition.

Let's see why do you need goals at a personal level.

WHY GOALS?

Why do you need goals? Or what is the need to set long-term, medium-term and short-term goals? Why not to just go with the flow?

Going with the flow is fine, but then you'll go wherever the flow goes. A person going with the flow is metaphorically like a boat without oars. The boat will go somewhere but not necessary where the person would have loved to go. And this is a passive way of living life by giving the control of your life to other people and circumstances.

Setting goals is like taking the charge of the boat and then sailing as hard as you can and aiming to reach where you want to go – not where others want you to go.

The goals give you a reason to act (or not act). They give you momentum, resilience, power, energy, self-worth and edge. A worthy goal can transform yours and the lives of others around you altogether.

Before starting the goal setting process

Before starting the process for yourself or others, I want you to keep few things in mind.

When most of us are planning, we get so engrossed in the process that it's not uncommon to set highly impractical goals, especially when we're in good mood or have experienced a recent success.

On the other hand, if someone has experienced a recent failure or rejection, divorce or is feeling low in energy due to any reason, it becomes very difficult to think about goals. If such person pushes himself to set goals, he may set very low goals.

We want a positive and relaxed state to set goal.

Also, when you're helping someone else, let's call them a client, set their goals, it's helpful for yourself to be in positive, relaxed and letting-go state. You need to be positive as the client will get influenced by your state. Hence, you should radiate positive energy during your interaction. Also, you need to be relaxed, because you don't want the client to physically tense himself while setting the goal. While doing this process it's important for you to be in a state of letting-go of all judgements and prejudices about the goals and the client's ability to achieve the goal.

TWO TYPES OF GOALS

For any result that you want to achieve - there are two types of goals.

1.   **Result/End goal:** The result goal or end goal is your ultimate aim in an endeavor. For example, getting six pack abs or retire by your 45th birthday, or being a millionaire by Dec 31, 2020 are examples of result goals. The result goals provide direction to your life.

2.   **The process goals:** The process goals help you reach your result goals. These are milestones that indicate whether you are on track to achieve a result goal or not? For example, to become a millionaire, you will need to have some milestones. For example, boosting your sales every quarter by certain percentage which will lead you to become a millionaire by Dec 31, 2020. And at the end of every quarter if you haven't achieved your process goal for that quarter, then you aren't on track to achieve your result goal.

THE WHEEL OF LIFE

If I ask you to set goals for your life, you may come up with a laundry list of things that you want in one or two particular areas. And often these are the lists of things that one is missing in their lives. For example, going to the gym more. Or spending more time in business and taking it to the next level. This is fine. The only issue is that these goals may not cover all aspects of your life. In Life Coaching we use a tool called Wheel of Life for goal setting. This tool gives a method to the goal setting process.

Here is how the wheel of life looks like.

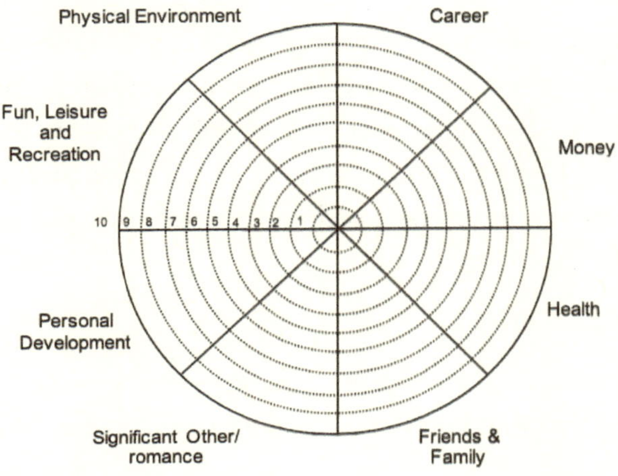

As you see, it's like a pie chart with multiple labels for each pie. The labels represent different areas of your life. There are multiple versions of this tool, some depicting lesser and others more areas. The example wheel of life has eight areas. Here is how to use it:

1.	Review each heading of the wheel of life.

2.	For each heading, rate your satisfaction level on a scale of 0-10, where 0 is no satisfaction at all and 10 is highest level of satisfaction.

3.	Write the number for each area and mark the level on circle.

4.	For each heading, fill the area between the satisfaction level and the center. For example, if your satisfaction level for personal development is 5– you will fill the area between center point and inner circle corresponding for level 5 in personal. By the end of the exercise you will have a nice pie chart of your areas.

5.   Now focus on the filled areas. If a perfect life had all levels at 10 and thus making a nice wheel of your satisfaction level, how balanced is your wheel now? Any new insights you have got? Which areas need more attention? If we were to give you this wheel to put it under the car of your life, how smooth your life will be?

This exercise would have given you some insights regarding the areas which you need to pay more attention to.

The amazing thing about the Wheel of Life is that all the areas are connected to each other. Hence, if you improve in one area, you'll experience improvements in other areas as well. Sometimes it may lead to decrease in scores in some areas as well. Hence, a periodic review of the Wheel of Life is important. NLP process of Well-Formed Outcome criteria helps you to avoid unwanted fluctuations by checking ecology during goal setting itself.

WELL-FORMED OUTCOMES CRITERIA

Over past few years, several goal setting methods have come into the field – the most popular of which is referred to as SMART criteria. SMART is an acronym that stands for specific, measurable, achievable, realistic and time-bound.

NLP has its own version of goal-setting criteria called NLP Well-Formed Outcomes criteria, which in my view is a much more holistic way of goal setting. It lays down a set of criteria which help ensure that your goal has higher chances of materializing. This also ensures that the goal is actually what you want.

There are several times that our clients do this process and decide upon a different goal because the original goal didn't feel right or didn't meet the ecology requirements.

This process can be used for result as well as process goals.

Positively Stated

The outcome should be positively stated. Most of the times the people are so much fed of their problems that they're clear about what they don't want – for example they may not want to get stuck in the job they don't like, they don't want to experience sadness etc.

However, having negative goals, i.e. the goals which focus on what a person doesn't want, is like going to a super market with the list of things you don't want to buy. It's overwhelming and lacks clarity.

Also, the mind cannot process negatives directly. Notice what happens when I say – "Don't think about the blue ball". In all cases the brain creates the picture of a blue ball, and then negates it. That means every time you think of something that you don't want, creates the imagery of that very thing in your mind.

Hence, people who don't want to go broke, are always broke. People who don't want bad relationships, end up having series of bad relationships. People who don't want the instability of career end up having unstable career.

Similarly, the goals which indicate losing or quitting are negative goals. For example, losing 15 kgs. of weight or quitting smoking are negatively stated. The mind doesn't like to lose anything.

To be effective your goal should be positively stated. Below are some examples of positively stated goals.

I want to become a millionaire by Dec 31, 2021.

I want to attain ideal weight of 60 Kgs, by Dec 31, 2020.

I want to experience healthy lungs, vitality and higher level of energy by Mar 31, 2020.

Questions to ask:

- *What do you want?*

- *What do you want instead?*

- *What would you rather have?*

Specify the context

The context of goal should be specified in as much detail as possible. By context of the goal we mean following three things:

- People

- Place

- Timeline

For example – "I want to own a 5000 square ft villa in a gated community in the heart of _________ city by Dec 31, 20__."

Questions:

- *What exactly do you want?*

- *Can you describe that more precisely?*

- *When do you want to achieve this goal?*

- *Where do you want to achieve this goal?*

- *Who else is a part of this goal?*

Self-Initiated and Self-Maintained

The commitment and motivation to do something is higher when the idea or goal originates from within you.

The outcome should be self-initiated and self-maintained. That is the inspiration to embark on journey, should be coming from within you and not because someone, e.g. your spouse or partner or someone else, wants you to achieve this goal.

Also, the outcome should be self- maintained. That in the process of achieving this outcome, you should not depend upon others as primary source of motivation. For example, let's say, you want to attain right weight of 65 Kg for yourself by Dec 31, 2018. But you are a person who sleeps late at night and only time you have got to go to the gym is in the morning. So, you are primarily dependent upon your spouse to get you up. Imagine, what would happen if the spouse also is unable to wake up early in the morning? What if the spouse has to go out of station?

Hence, it's equally important for a goal to be self-maintained as it is to be self-initiated for you to have highest odds in your favor.

Questions to ask:

- *How far this goal is under your control?*

- *Are you doing it for yourself or for someone else?*

- *Does the outcome rely solely on you?*

- *What are you going to do?*

- *What will you be doing to achieve this goal?*

- *What can you offer others that will also make them want to help you?*

Evidence

By evidence we mean, that you should know:

1. Whether you have achieved the goal

2. Whether you are on the right track to achieve the goal

You should have the main goal and then milestones or mini-goals which lead towards that goal. The main goal is easy to verify. However, milestones are very crucial, especially for medium- and long-term goals. They provide you a feedback mechanism about whether you are on track for your goal. Well placed milestones and their periodic review help you to make any course corrections if required.

Questions to ask:

- *How will you know that you are getting the desired outcome?*

- *What will you be doing when you get it?*

- *What will you see, hear and feel when you have it?*

- *How will you know that you have achieved your goal?*

- *What milestones will you set up along the way?*

- *How will you know that you are on track for this goal?*

- *How often will you check that you are on track?*

Resource Check

Take a stock of your internal and external resources.

Internal Resources: Internal resources are resources which are inside you like confidence, motivation, life experiences, intuition, insights etc.

External Resources: External resources are resources which come from the environment outside you and help you in attaining your goal. For example, trainings, mentoring, books, CD/DVDs, finances etc.

Questions to ask:

- *What resources you will need to achieve that goal?*

- *What resources do you have now?*

- *What resources do you need to acquire?*

- *Where will you find the resources you need?*

- *What happens if you act as if you have the* resources?

Chunking/Appropriate Size

Is the outcome correct size? The size of the outcome decides out motivation levels.

If the size of the outcome is too big then you may feel overwhelmed. In such a situation, you must chunk it down in smaller outcomes. In such case ask yourself:

What prevents me from having this outcome?

And whatever problems or obstacles you come up with, reframe them as smaller outcomes.

On the other hand, if the size of the outcome is too small, you may not feel motivated enough to work towards it. In such case chunk it up by asking:

What will having this outcome do for me?

Keep chunking up until you relate it to an outcome that is sufficiently big and motivating.

Ecology

Many people spend their lifetimes climbing the ladder of success, only to realize upon reaching the top that it was leaning against the wrong wall. In NLP's world, this type of outcome is called a well-formed outcome. It must be ecological. Ecological in simplest terms means good for everyone involved.

For example, taking up a long-term travelling assignment in order to be a millionaire by the next 10 years, to be able to spend quality time with family is an inspiring outcome, but may not be ecological if you already have a family and children are young right now. In 10 years the kids would have grown up and may not be able to relate to you as a parent with whom they love to spend time. You would have missed out their childhood years.

Similarly, going on for an intensive workout regime to lose 30 Kg in 3 months may be aspiring but not ecological as you may end up hurting yourself.

An ecological goal is the one which is good for you, for others around you, the environment and doesn't need compromising on other goals of your life.

Questions to ask:

- *What is the real purpose why you want this?*

- *What will you lose or gain if you get it?*

- *What are the consequences for the other people?*

- *What would your significant other and family members think of the goals?*

- *What is the cost in time, money and opportunity?*

- *What might you need to give up?*

- *How will the balance between the different aspects of your life be affected when you are working towards this outcome?*

- *How will the balance between the different aspects of your life be affected when you achieve this outcome?*

- *What is important in your present circumstances that you might have to leave behind?*

Preserve the underlying positive intention

This is based upon the NLP Presupposition that for any behavior there is underlying positive intention. Similarly, your current situation is also fulfilling some underlying positive intention. We have to take care of this underlying positive intention, else there is always a possibility of falling back to the current state.

For example, let's say, someone wants to quit smoking. The smoking might be giving that person relaxation, opportunity to become social etc. No matter how determined the person is or how many NLP techniques you use on that person, if you don't take care of these underlying intentions then this person may have temporary change and then be back to the square one.

Questions to ask:

- *What are the underlying positive intentions that your current situation is fulfilling for you?*

- *How will you ensure that these positive intentions are taken care of when you are working towards your goal?*

- *How will you ensure that these positive intentions are taken care of once you have your goal?*

Do you still want it?

After going through all the questions, it is likely that due to some reason you may not want to have the goal for some or other reason, or want to modify it. Hence ask yourself:

- *Do you still want to have it?*

If the answer to this question is yes then move on to the next question.

Next Action/First step

If the answer to previous question is yes, then:

- *What is the first step that you can take towards your goal?*

The first step can be a small step like buying a book that you identified in resource check, as an external resource that you need to have. Or it could be talking to someone who has achieved similar goal in past. The key is to have the first step something that is appropriate size which you can finish in lesser time. We are just aiming our mind towards the goal.

It's all about well-formed outcomes. As you might have noticed various steps in this goal setting make it more comprehensive than the goal setting in other methodologies.

Also, you may not be able to finish the whole process off in a single sitting. Very often we spend 2-3 sessions in helping the client set their goals as per the well-formed outcomes. In these sessions the client sets main goal as per the well-formed outcomes. And then we work on the milestones which would lead the client to the goal. Then each of these milestones are also run through well-formed outcomes criteria. It's sometimes a long process, but worth spending time – only 5% people in the world know clearly what they want. Rest 95% are just going with the flow. The 5% who have clearly defined goals – have the higher chance of reaching what they want to. The others, will reach "somewhere".

CHAPTER 11
BEING CERTAIN ABOUT YOUR GOAL

It's easier to set goals, but difficult to follow through. This is the reason that most of new year resolutions fail. You may attribute this to lack of motivation. However, many times the people aren't motivated because they are not certain about their ability to achieve the goals.

It's very important to be convinced that the goal is achievable. If you're certain that you can win 100 meters race, you will have strong motivation to practice harder and harder.

The following process helps you to be certain about your goal.

BEING CERTAIN ABOUT YOUR GOAL

1. Think about something you are certain about, maybe what did you have for breakfast today?
2. Notice where does the image shows up in your mind's eye and its Submodalities.
3. Shake your body.
4. Think about something else that you're certain about, maybe what did you have for lunch yesterday?
5. Check the similarities between both images.
6. Try this on couple of more memories to be sure about the Submodalities of things you are certain about.

7. Now think of your goal and notice where the image shows up.
8. Now use your hands and pull the image to put it in the same location where the images of things you are certain about show up.
9. Make the Submodalities of the goal image same as the things you are certain about.
10. Break state.
11. Test – think about the goal again. Notice the location of the images and how do you feel about the goal.

CHAPTER 12
WALT DISNEY STRATEGY

Now that you have got your goal figured out, it's time to refine it and look at it from all perspectives. One way to look at the goals is to always treat them as dynamic rather than static. Your big vision should be very high. However, life isn't predictable. So, feel comfortable in doing adjustments as and when required to your goal.

In this chapter you're going to learn a powerful technique of refining and re-defining your goals, modelled after Walt Disney's strategies.

WALT-DISNEY PROCESS- INTRODUCTION TO THREE PERSONALITIES

Walt Disney had a profound strategy to handle his projects. He used to exhibit three types of behaviors.

1. The Dreamer
2. The Realist
3. The Critic

It's helpful to think of these behaviors as three personalities.

The Dreamer, sees opportunities whenever he sees a problem. He thinks about grand solutions to problems. He thinks about creating revolution in the world through a single idea. Steve Jobs is a great example of a dreamer. Since beginning of his life Steve Jobs thought on the lines of "creating a dent in the universe".

"We are here to put a dent in the universe. Otherwise why else even be here?" – Steve Jobs

It's difficult to stop a dreamer when he's on the roll. He can go on and on about a seemingly simple idea. He can see potential in simple things.

The Realist, thinks about practical aspects. If the dreamer builds castles in the air, the realist creates plans to bring these castles down to the earth, trim them here and there so that things fit the available resources and finally puts foundations under them. The managers in an organization are realists. Regardless of what their Job Description in a company says, the managers' role is to bring predictability in the organization. Their mantra is to not fix anything unless it's broken.

The critic is a highly intellectual part who can look at things from all angles and come up with a number of scenarios where a goal may fail. The job of the critic is to review a goal and provide honest comments. Here it's important to consider that the critic doesn't have negative connotations in this process. The role of the critic is to look into the plans and expose the loopholes so as to avoid unnecessary risks or debacles.

We all have a bit of these personalities. However, we may not be using them in a correct way. For example, we may be overtly dreamers when we think of our future, realist when we go and buy a car and a critic when we have to deal with our spouses or many times when we analyze our past debacles.

Walt Disney is said to exhibit all three personalities in the context of his work.

When a new idea popped into his head, he would behave like a dreamer on a roll. Thinking and talking highly about the transformation that this idea is going to bring in the world. Here everything would look rosy. He would create really BIG vision for what he wanted to achieve through this idea.

After this, he would start working on the plan. Here, he would show up like a realistic – creating plans, managing resource and making sure things work as per the plan.

While working on the plan, he would also show up like a critic – thinking about scenarios where things may go wrong, finding faults, loopholes etc. Before we go forward, most of us have negative notions about the word 'critic'. We shouldn't undermine or detest it. The critic's role is to help to refine the plan, and not to sabotage the process.

Now let's go through the process.

HOW TO USE THE DISNEY STRATEGY?

The Disney Strategy is useful in refining your goals/plans. This process has two phases:

Phase 1: Spatially Anchoring the Dreamer, Realist and the Reviewer/Critic

Phase 2: Refining the plan using these anchors.

Also, in the step 2, realize that all three parts are inside you. They must discuss the plan and not criticize each other's behavior. In real world the realist may scorn at the critic. People tend to avoid them. However, in Disney Strategy all three parts have equal status. They are used constructively.

DISNEY STRATEGY PROCESS

• Think about the goal you want to convert into a plan.

• Identify three points on the floor which are neither too far and nor too close. The may be like the three corners of a triangle.

• Anchor the dreamer: Go to the first point. Think about a time when you were at your best in creating vision. Once the memory comes to the mind, go to the memory as if it's happening now. Make the pictures bigger, brighter and colorful. Now leave this feeling here and step out of the point. Break state. Test by re-entering the dreamer space.

• Anchor the realist: Now think about a time when you made wonderful plans in any context. It may be your personal or professional life. Once the memory comes to the mind, go to the memory as if it's happening now. Make the pictures bigger, brighter and colorful. Now leave this feeling here and step out of the point. Break state. Test by re-entering the realist space.

• Anchor the critic space: Think about a time when you constructively criticized something, and the criticism contributed to improvement. Once the memory comes to the mind, go to the memory as if it's happening now. Make the pictures bigger, brighter and colorful. Now leave this feeling here and step out of the point. Break state. Test by re-entering the critic space.

• Dream big: Think about the goal you want to work on and enter the dreamer space. Here let your imagination go loose. Dream big, create grand visions etc.

- Plan: Now go to the realist place. And create a plan to make the dream happen.

- Find loopholes: Now go to the critic space. Look at the plan from all angles. Find the loopholes and possible scenarios where the plan would fail.

- Constructive interaction: Now in response to the points you came up with in the last step, move between dreamer and realist intuitively, each iteration should refine the plan further. Here it's important to remember that all three parts are discussing the plan. They should discuss plan only and not any particular part's behavior.

Continue iterations: Now keep on moving between dreamer, realist and critic without following any pre-defined order, till the plan is refined in such a way that the critic has no other point to make.

CHAPTER 13
MAKING THE GOAL WORK AT SUBCONSCIOUS LEVEL

Once you have created your goal, refined the plan with Walt-Disney process – it's time to increase your chances of achieving it. NLP has a beautiful process called Visual Squash for Goal Integration. It provides a pathway for the subconscious mind to work towards the goal.

VISUAL SQUASH FOR GOAL INTEGRATION

- Sit in a comfortable place

- Extend your left and right hands in front of you with palms facing upwards, elbows bent and not touching the body and there should be comfortable gap of about 2-3 feet between both hands.

- Your left hand represents your present state and right hand is the state where you want to reach i.e. after the goal is achieved.

- Present your present self on your left hand. Make the picture bigger, brighter, and as much detailed as you can.

- Present yourself after achieving the goal on your right hand. Again make the picture bigger, brighter and as much detailed as you can.

- Imagine there is an invisible path in semi arched or rainbow shape between your left to right hand side.

• Now think about 3-5 steps which will lead you from the left hand state to the right hand state. What pictures come to your mind? Select one picture for each step.

• Now put these pictures in chronological order along the semi arched path.

• Bring your attention to the first step. Make the picture representing this step bigger, brighter and add more details. Notice if you can hear some sounds. If you hear them, make the sounds more pleasant to hear. Feel how you will feel at this step.

o Do this process for every step one by one

• By now you would have 3-5 slides or pictures in a chronological sequence so that the each slide on left leads to the slide after this.

• Imagine the path from left hand to right hand side is illuminated.

• Now slowly and steadily bring your hands together, on the way compressing the pictures together.

• Notice how each movement of hands moving close to each other feels. You may feel tingling or energetic pressure.

• Join both hands and squash all images together.

• Now press both hands palms against your chest and let things integrate.

CHAPTER 14
BOOSTING YOUR SELF-ESTEEM

Your self-esteem is a very important factor into your success. People with high self-esteem have been found to be more successful in life. They are virtually unstoppable. Regardless of their life circumstances they can turn things around in their favor.

However, people with poor self-esteem are opposite. They have to work harder and longer to achieve the same amount of happiness and success as the people with high self-esteem. Also, even if life presents them immense amount of success, by chance happenings, they mostly give all of that up very soon.

Hence, it's important for you to develop a very high self-esteem. In this chapter you're going to learn techniques for boosting your self-esteem.

SELF-APPRECIATION

We are socially conditioned to suppress expressing appreciation towards ourselves. There are high chances that like most of people, you're programmed by your parents and society to downplay our achievements.

This lack of self-acknowledgement keeps building up and later on results in physical, mental and/or emotional issues.

Hence, you should learn to appreciate yourself for your own health and well-being.

Self-Appreciation exercise

1.   Calibrate you level of self-appreciation on a scale of 0-10, 0 being total absence of self-appreciation and 10 being highest level of self-appreciation.

2.   Think of someone who you know loves and accepts you unconditionally. It can be a living or dead person. It can even be a pet, if you will. For our exercise we would like to call it "loving being".

3.   Now sit on a chair and close your eyes. Imagine that there is a golden notebook in your lap and a golden pen. This notebook is your autobiography.

4.   Imagine that you're writing your autobiography. And as you're doing so, imagine the "loving being" standing at some distance behind a plexi-glass and looking at you. They're presence cannot disturb you or interfere in your work.

5.   See how this person looks as he is looking at you with total unconditional love and acceptance.

6.   Now imagine leaving your body on chair and floating from your chair landing next to the "loving being".

7.   Look at the "loving being" who is looking at you sitting on the chair and admiring you. Notice the body language, posture etc. of the person.

8.   Now go ahead and step into the body of the "loving being". Look from his eyes, hear from his ears and feel the feeling of admiration and unconditional acceptance.

9.   From inside the body of the "loving being" look at the part of you sitting on the chair and writing autobiography. Notice - What does this "loving being" see in you? What does this "loving being" think about you? And also notice, what are the qualities in you that this loving being admires.

10.   Now carry the feelings of the "loving being" and float out of his body and stand next to him. Look at you with the same level of admiration and love.

11.   Float from this position and come back into your body carrying the feelings of appreciation, acceptance and love that you just learned.

12.   Write down various qualities in your golden notebook, which you learned about yourself from previous steps while being in the body of the "loving being" and then being a watcher next to him.

13.   Once you are done, come back to the room and open your eyes.

14.   Break state.

15.   Test your level of self-appreciation.

Repeat this exercise as many times as possible, until the feeling of self-appreciation becomes integral part of you in all contexts of life.

It's also recommended that you repeat this exercise for different contexts in life e.g. career, relationship, social etc. to make sure the highest level of self-appreciation in all areas of your life.

SELF-ESTEEM BOOSTER

As the life goes by, not everything is going to be perfect. Something somewhere may and will go wrong. Even if it's a small petty thing, after a number of repetitions you might end up criticizing yourself. This isn't good for your well-being.

The following exercise takes care of this by following the "prevention is better than cure" advice.

One should do this after any activity which hasn't gone completely well. For example, a small snag in your presentation in front of your team etc. This may or may not seem overtly harmful. Still you must do this exercise.

1.   Think about the event that just happened. Make a mental movie of the event and take a stock of things which went well and didn't go so well.

2.   Calibrate your level of satisfaction with this even on a scale of 0-10.

3.   What resources could have helped you in this situation?

4.   Anchor these resources on different parts of your body.

5.   Now fire first anchor and take that resource and relive the memory of the event in new way.

6.   Break state.

7.   Do this for each resource one by one, with each iteration separated by a break state.

8.   Break state.

9.   Now calibrate your level of satisfaction with the new memory of the event.

10.   Close the session, if the level of satisfaction is 10 out of the 10.

11.   If the level of satisfaction is less than 10, repeat the process from step #3 by identifying the other possible resources which could have helped you in the situation.

HANDLING CRITICISM

One of the biggest blows to a person's self-esteem is continuous criticism by the others - especially coming from the authority figures or peers whose acceptance we seek.

The following technique helps you to stay resourceful in the face of such criticism.

1.   Think about some incident in which someone criticized you.

2.   In front of you make an imaginary circle in which the process is going to happen. Project your *self* who was criticized and now want to learn new way of dealing with the criticism. Imagine the incident happening there in the circle.

3.   Imagine this *self* in a protective shield of plexi-glass, so as to dissociate itself from the criticism.

4.   Watch as that *self* makes a movie of what the criticizer is saying. What does the criticizer mean? Does that *self* has enough information to make a clear, detailed picture? If the answer is "yes," proceed to the next step, else gather more information.

5.   Let that *self* decide on response. For example it could agree with part of criticism which is rational or just excuse itself by saying "I will think over it" etc.

6.   Ask that self if it wants to use the information it got from the criticism to act somewhat differently next time? If yes, how would it like to behave next time? Ask it to make a mental movie of the new behavior, and then experience it by stepping into it.

7.   Having watched the movie, would you like this behavior that your *self* depicted for yourself? If no, then how would you like to modify that strategy in a better way? If yes, then proceed to the next step.

8.   Thank that *self* for being a resource to you in learning the new response. Now, move forward into the circle and step into that self. Allow this self to integrate with you.

9.   Break state.

10.   Future pace.

CHAPTER 15
CREATING NEW BEHAVIORS TO FULFILL YOUR GOAL

A person is a slave of their habits. Good or bad, habits form a comfort zone for all of us. It's easier to stay with a habit than to change it. That is the reason why people keep smoking, getting up late, getting into useless patterns in life etc.

Some of these behaviors support your goal and plan. However, many behaviors don't support you in fulfilling your plans or goals that you have. These need to be changed such that they support you in achieving your goal. In this chapter you're going to learn some awesome NLP techniques using which you can easily and effortlessly change your behaviors.

Identify current behaviors/Habits which need to be changed

Before you go further, I invite you to take your pen and notepad and list out all behaviors and habits which you currently have and may hinder you goal.

Now think - which of these behaviors, you would like to change first? And what behavior you would like to have instead?

A behavior may be useful in one context but as your situations change the behavior may need to be changed as well.

I've always been a late-night person. It served me well since my college days. However, when my son started going to school, I had to get up early in the morning. Since I would sleep late, the moment the alarm used to go off I used to get up disgruntled. I didn't like this part of the day. The way you start your day can have a cascading effect on most of your day. I decided that a more useful behavior for me would be to wake up in peaceful manner when the alarm goes off. And I did steal a skill NLP technique and have been getting up peacefully for about half a decade now. The old behavior of being disgruntled in the morning hasn't returned yet.

STEAL A SKILL TECHNIQUE

1.   Think about the behavior you want to change.

2.   Think about how you would like to behave instead.

3.   Now, think of someone who you know does the new behavior you identified wonderfully. You should have seen this person doing this behavior either in real or through video.

4.   Now close your eyes and imagine this person doing the new behavior. Notice the body language, muscle movements, the way of speaking etc.

5.   Imagine floating out of your body and entering into the person's body. See from the eyes of the person, hear from their ears, and feel how does it feel when you depict this behavior from inside the body of the person.

6.   Learn the new behavior by doing it while inside the body of the person.

7.   Now imagine floating out of the body of the person and back into your body carrying all the learning.

8.   Allow yourself to learn the new learnings.

9.   Break state.

10.   Now, think about a situation in which you would have behaved in the other way.

11.   Imagine being into that situation and notice what happens. You should notice automatically performing new behavior.

12.   Repeat the process in case you see yourself doing your old behavior in previous step. You may take another role model.

You can use the above technique for let's say, becoming a better speaker, trainer, coach or therapist. Anything is possible as long as you have the visual representation of a model doing this behavior.

Complex scenarios

Now, you may want to have a behavior which have multiple components and you may not have a single role model doing all of them. For example, you may want to become a better parent or a more successful businessman, who has several qualities, but you may not know anyone who has got all of these qualities.

In that case you can repeat the previous process by identifying a role model for each of the desired qualities and repeating the process for each role model.

Another way is to imagine, all your role models coming together and showing their behaviors one by one. Then allow them to merge together into one personality. And do the new behavior generator with the new personality.

The human mind is a wonderful imagination machine. What is great about it is that it cannot differentiate between the reality and imagination.

That means the new behavior generator can be done with an imagined personality as well in case you don't have any actual visual representation of the person doing the behavior. However, for several reasons I would prefer a real role model as much as possible.

SWISH PATTERN

Swish is a really cool technique to change a behavior which has a trigger associated with it. For example, every time you want to take a small break, you may be going to a particular website and then start browsing. This isn't a behavior that you want as it's taking away your time.

Swish is a technique which is helpful in changing the behaviors which has an identifiable trigger. For example, in above example the trigger is the thought of relaxing. Using Swish you can program your mind to respond differently when the same trigger happens next time.

1.   Think about the behavior that you want to get rid of. Notice which image comes to your mind. This is your **cue image**.

2.   Think about the trigger for this behavior. In above example, the trigger is thought of relaxing in the middle/start of work.

3.   Think what it would be like without this behavior. Notice the image that comes to your mind. Make this image brighter, more colorful and bigger.

1.   Now dissociate from this image if you have got associated into it.

2.   Shrink it into the size of a dot. As the image shrinks, imagine, all colors in image getting condensed and finally you have a grey dot.

3.   Now place this grey dot at the bottom left corner of the cue image (step 1)

4.   This is your setup.

4.   Bring the setup to mind. Mentally count from 1…2…3 and think about the trigger and setup. And immediately make the sound of SWIIIIIIIISH or WOOOOOOOOSH. As you make the sound imagine the colored cue image shrinking and turning grey, and at the same time imagine the grey dot at the bottom left corner expanding and turning into a fully colored, bright and big image.

5.   Repeat the previous step 3-5 times.

6.   Break state: shift your body or distract yourself in some other way.

7.   Test: Think about the trigger and notice how the image and behavior has changed. If you still feel there are some traces of the old behavior do SWISH few more times.

GODIVA CHOCOLATE PATTERN

Godiva Chocolate Pattern is a wonderful technique to change your feelings about someone or something. An example is going to gym. If you've never been to gym or associate pain with going to gym, then you need to reprogram your mind to associate pleasure with going to gym. Here is Godiva Chocolate Technique for feeling motivated.

1. Create an intense and associated picture of something that you really love or are compelled to do. For example, you may not be able to resist reading new self-help book, or maybe some food etc.

2. Break state.

3. Create a picture of something towards which you want to feel motivated - such as going to gym, cleaning up, paperwork, etc.

4. Make the first picture (motivated) big enough so that it can cover the second picture (of the thing you have trouble starting) and keep it over the second picture – such that you can see only the picture of the thing you feel motivated about and the picture of the thing that you resist is behind it.

5. As you look at the picture of the thing that you cannot resist, feel the feelings of not being able to resist and allow them to increase. As the feeling reaches its peak, imagine that a tiny hole opens up in the middle of the first picture, and that allows you to have a small peek at the picture behind it. Have a look at the second picture for few seconds and then close the hole and let the feeling of motivation and not being able to resist peak again.

6. Now repeat previous step again and again each time allowing the hole to be bigger than previous iteration.

7. Break state.

8. Test: Think about the thing you resisted earlier. How do you feel about it now? Repeat the process if there are still some traces left.

CIRCLE OF EXCELLENCE

Circle of Excellence is a powerful process which can get you into the most powerful states instantaneously. For example, imagine that you're a salesperson and had a crucial appointment with a high-profile customer. You leave from your home such that you can arrive there 30 minutes before the appointment and freshen yourself. However, you get stuck in the traffic and are just able to reach the office of the client at the time of appointment. You don't have the time to freshen up. And you must immediately rush to meet the client. The circle of excellence can be your savior in such cases. I have used this technique many times for myself to switch my state from say working on writing this book to making a sales call and then back to writing.

Here is how it goes:

•   Think about the internal resources you would need to achieve your goal.

•   Think about a time in the past when you had this resource in some other situation. For example, if you want to feel more confident around people, you can think of a time when you felt highly confident let's say while playing some video game. The context is different, but we're after confidence.

•   Imagine there is a medium sized circle in front of you on the floor – big enough such that you can comfortably stand in it.

•   Step into this circle and think of the time when you felt really confident. Imagine as if it's happening now. Use the same body posture, make the picture bigger and brighter, adjust the sounds, add more details. Feel the intensity of confidence rising.

- Now leave this state in the circle and step back. How are you feeling now? You might notice that the state is no longer with you.

- Look at the circle and notice the color of the circle. Is it rotating? If yes, what is the speed? Adjust the speed, and if change the color if you would like to.

- Once you are satisfied, just step into the circle again and test it. You should feel the feeling of confidence surging up inside you.

- Now, step back again from circle. Use your imagination and hands and collect all the color of the circle and make a bracelet or some other ornament out of it. Wear it in your hand. This bracelet represents your circle of excellence. Whenever you need to get into the state of confidence - all that you need to do is take off this bracelet and throw it in front of you. Like a sci-fi movie, it will expand into your circle of excellence and all that you have to do is step into it.

- Test this. Throw this bracelet out at some part of room and step into it.

Also, you need not bother to put this bracelet back. It will automatically come back to your wrist after you're done with the circle of excellence in any situation.

CHAPTER 16
DEVELOP THE VOICE OF INFLUENCE

You voice is perhaps the most powerful persuasive tool you have available. If you don't use your voice right, you'll find that no matter what you say, it will not be heard, understood and acted upon. As per some studies, the measure of how much someone likes someone is determined far more by their tone of voice than by almost any other single factor.

NLP has number of tools for influence. Use your voice correctly and you'll find that even if you mistake other influence tools you will still be able to be influential. No matter how badly you may mess up a persuasive pattern from NLP, a story or even the entire structure of what you're saying, you will still sound convincing and confident. People will still respond to you the way you want them to.

Voice is incredibly powerful and so often overlooked tool of influence. Many people concentrate on just the language patterns like Milton Model. And they ignore the voice modulation. It is as if the language pattern would do the job. That is not true. Have you heard someone poorly mimicking a popular movie dialogue? How was the audience response? How was your response? On the other hand, Sometimes, the dialogue delivery makes an average dialogue a masterpiece act. You can see this time and again in comedy shows or drama.

In today's world where many of deals are happening over phone or over audio conference, it is imperative to have high quality voice. And it can be easily done as you will learn in this chapter.

Let us start with the basics and see how to create an influential voice?

MIND YOUR VOICE ORIGIN

First step of developing the Voice of Influence is to originate the voice from right place.

The voice can originate from many places in your body – from head, nose, mouth, throat, lungs, or belly reason. When we say originate – we can also interpret it as reverberate. Sometimes, we say that so and so singer is a nasal singer or that singer sings from his nose. In this case nose area of that person vibrates more than the chest or belly area.

In case of influence the lower in the body you go while speaking the more influential the voice is. Here is an exercise to differentiate between different types of voices and to fine tune your voice to originate from correct place.

Exercise

1.   Place you hand on your head, focus your attention where you hand is touching your head and speak from this place – This is the voice from my head.

2.   Place a finger on your nose tip, focus on where your finger is touching your nose and say – This is the voice from my nose.

3.   Place your hand on your mouth, focus on your mouth and say – This is the voice from my mouth.

4.   Place your hand on your throat, focus on the touch and say – This is the voice from my throat.

5.   Place your hand on your chest, focus on the touch and say – This is the voice from my chest.

6.   Place your hand on your belly, focus all your attention on the touch and say – This is the voice from my belly. This is how the voice of influence sound like. I love this voice. As long as I have this voice I can influence as many people as I want.

This is where you should speak from. Dedicate few minutes every day to practice belly speaking. It will sound odd initially if you are not used to it. Just go with it.

If you're a man, there should be sort of a resonant and rumbly quality and if you're a woman, it should just sound deep, controlled and powerful.

Also, the when you speak in this way, you will notice you are automatically taking deeper breaths and while speaking throwing more air out. The rate of speech will also be slower for naturally fast speakers.

Having said that, let us now look at the rate of speech.

REGULATING THE RATE OF SPEECH

Too many people, in a conversation or influence setting, are nervous. They want to rush to throw the words out of their mouth, lest they forget them on the way. This automatically makes them to take smaller breaths and speak from higher up in the body, thereby reducing the quality of their voice.

The be influential, you need to talk as low in the body as possible and at low rate. This may seem to be counter intuitive. So many people mistake sharpness with the speed of voice. Listen to recordings of influential people from Internet. Some names you may want to listen to are Mahatma Gandhi, Martin Luther King Jr, Bill Clinton, Barack Obama etc. These are names from past and present century covering almost 100 years of history. One common thing you will notice in all of them is that their rate of speech is far slower than other leaders. Now increase their rate of speech to 125%. What do you notice? You may notice that they do not sound as influential as before. Now increase the rate of speech to 150% or 200% and observe what happens. Are they still influential?

Hence the second tool is to regulate your rate of speech so that you speak 25% slower than average person. This may sound odd in the beginning to the fast speakers.

However, you may think about the highly motivational speakers who are known to speak forcefully and fast. Many great motivators are known to use this strategy. However, that is on purpose. And they are still speaking from the belly. And you would notice that after few high-speed lines – these speakers abruptly drop their rate of speech, creating more impact on the audience.

To be effective your rate has to be optimum as per your audience. A very slow speech to very brainy audience will bore them down just as a very fast speech will lose its impact.

SPEAKING IN RHYTHM

Now again listen to the speeches you listened before. You may notice a rhythm in their voice, as if there is a hidden melody.

The influential speakers never speak in monotonous voice. You must keep varying the tone and rhythm while talking. Initially you may tend to focus on rhythm if you are not used to it. This may hamper the communication.

The best way to do this is to practice alone while reading something. And while you are doing this exercise, experiment with putting gaps or varying rates of speech at various parts of the sentences.

And when you are with others, just go with normal flow of conversation. With time, you the practice patterns will automatically start showing up in your normal day to day conversation.

DELIVERING IMPORTANT POINTS

In your paragraph or sentence will have important message points. These are the key points around which your speech is woven. When you are at these points, change your voice tonality and rhythm to mark them to the subconscious mind of the person.

For example, you may deepen your voice, or raise it and reduce the speed of speech drastically. You may also speak each word in that part of sentence with a stress as if you are bouncing off each word. The subconscious mind of the other person will take mark this as important command.

This is why the embedded commands work.

SMILE WHILE TALKING

This one is very important especially when you are talking on phone.

It's often been said that when speaking on the phone to somebody, it's very hard to get your message across because they don't know how you're feeling.

That's actually not true. If you smile when you're on the phone, people will pick up the smile.

When you smile, the entire nature of the way you sound, of the way you shape your words, comes out completely differently.

While commuting long distance, sometimes I put FM and listen to the famous RJ's. Try doing this next time you are driving. Their voices are well modulated. And they speak in rhythm. And at the same time always you will notice they seem to be smiling when they are talking, enjoying every moment of talking. And the audience picks up that smile and enjoyment. The role of RJ is sometimes more important as the choice of songs on the program. There are many people who listen to these programs just to listen to RJ's conversation.

Word of caution is not to overdo it. And do this in the appropriate context. It is common sense not to smile while offering condolences.

USING POWER OF PAUSE

Nothing builds suspense than an artful pause. Make use of this pattern.

When you pause while speaking, when you stop, hold eye contact, because it lets people know that you are in control. They feel you know what you're doing, you are the master of yourself. At subconscious level, they think that what you say has importance, deserves attention and mental focus. That is the power of pause.

Varying Speed Artfully: Charisma Pattern

This part is related to speed itself – and I call it "The Charisma Pattern". I invite you again to listen to some parts of the influential people's recordings. You will notice a pattern which is very common.

They speed up while talking and then slow down… then speed up again and slow down again. It is like pump action.

Practice this when alone. Use it during your conversations and presentation.

By speeding up the way you speak and slowing down, you're doing what many of the greatest politicians like Martin Luther King Jr., Barack Obama and even Adolf Hitler used to do.

And this one simple pattern, that of slowing down and speeding up as you talk, makes you far more compelling, far more persuasive.

When you speak fast, it raises your energy as well as the audience's energy. When you pause, you convert this energy into suspense energy. When you slow down, you can embed powerful commands in that part of the sentence thereby making them more effective. Or even if you do not embed any commands there, people will feel engaged. It will be soothing for them. The energy will go down, but not for far too long as you will start speeding up. It is like the Bull Market stock index graph you see very often. The market goes up and then pauses and breathes (goes down), and then again goes up with far more force and to far higher levels.

This is the power of charisma pattern.

Combine the Charisma Pattern with projecting from your diaphragm, smiling when appropriate and using pauses powerfully, and you will discover that you can speak with the voice of a master persuader and somebody who is phenomenally influential.

CHAPTER 17
USE THE POWER OF EMBEDDED COMMANDS

Embedding commands is a technique to impress the subconscious mind of the listener during normal conversation.

It is based upon the fact that the subconscious mind is far more alert to small variations than the conscious mind. This is part of development of the human mind.

For example, while you are driving, you might be consciously talking to your friend sitting next to you and yet reach your destination after taking so many turns on the way. And many of the turns you took, you would not even remember them. This is subconscious mind in action. While the conscious mind is chatting, the subconscious mind is paying attention to other details on the road.

The same happens during the normal conversation. The conscious mind is focusing on the content all the time. At the same time the subconscious mind is paying attention to a lot of stuff, for example, the variations in voice tonality and body language.

Milton Erickson used this fact to great advantage. Embedding commands is one of the most profound aspects of Ericksonian Hypnosis. The client's conscious mind would be engaged in deciphering the meaning of the language patterns, which would keep coming at him at a high rate. As the conscious mind of the client would have got immensely entangled in the content, Erickson would simultaneously be talking to the subconscious mind of the client using Embedded Commands, by varying his voice tone. This variation of the voice tone was too subtle for the conscious mind to notice. However, the subconscious mind would catch this shift in tonality and respond to the suggestion. And after the session the client would have become a changed person.

Varying Voice Tonality

By now, you would have realized that Embedding Command by varying the voice tonality is going to be a very powerful tool in your hands while persuading someone.

So how do you do that?

In English, there are three types of voice tonalities with which you end the sentences.

In first type you keep the same tone throughout the sentence. The sentences said with this style are interpreted as statements.

For example, say this aloud, but naturally – Paris is in France.

If you spoke correctly, you would have spoken this sentence in monotone.

Now say this: Aurangabad is India, isn't it? Or Is Aurangabad in India?

Here towards the end of the sentence the voice inflection is upwards. This is questioning tonality.

Now say this: Hey close that door! Or Come here! (as if you are asking your pet to come)

Here towards the end of the sentence the voice inflection is downwards. This is command tonality. Again, say this and note the voice quality. Keep this quality in mind, because this that what you will need to embed command.

In section Analog Marking we are going to discuss some more ways to mark the embedded commands.

Steps To Embed Commands

Here are steps for beginners:

- Decide what commands do you want to embed

- Decide in what kind of context you can embed them.

- Take the conversation in that context and start embedding the commands at appropriate places.

During normal conversations, you will have far lesser time to make first two decisions i.e. deciding embedded commands and context. And sometimes you will not be able to change the context as well. At that time, the things should come out spontaneously and with little tweaking of the context.

How to do that? This is the same question I faced when I started with NLP. All that I did was to *keep practicing* the embedded commands what I was alone and when talking to my friends and family members. With time I got a hang of it. Afterwards it became easier to *talk to anyone and embed commands*. You can also do the same. *Start practicing* with your friends and family. Change the direction of the conversation in your favor. In the beginning, you can start with telling stories and while telling the stories you can *embed the commands* through some character's dialogue. For example, and then the prince said," *You are beautiful.* I have come from hundred miles to see you. And I had heard about how beautiful you are and that *you are super-confident.* I am glad that I have found you. You are all that I had heard about you and much more. I need to go now; however, you *relax yourself* because I will be back soon."

Now carefully re-read the last paragraph aloud, starting from – How to do that? And everywhere you find italics, that is an embedded command. This is simple, isn't it?

So, the best way to embed commands for beginners is by telling a story. It can be something that happened with you, or someone else, or it could be a story which you heard from somewhere. And it could just be a made-up-on-the-fly story as well. The issue is not how good or true the story is, but how relevant it is in the context to do the deep work.

Just when you come to the italicized text say it with command tonality and then continue with the rest of the conversation in your normal tone.

Will People Detect It?

You may be wondering, what if people find this out. And I would say that people are too engrossed in their own world. Initially do it sparingly and see how they react. Then slowly increase frequency. And you will be amazed that when you are doing it in right way, you will be able to get away with a lot of things. Most of the time people will not be able to notice it. And at other times they will give you the benefit of doubt and move on.

Caution

One caution however is not to try your luck too far. If you suggest something against the other person's value or beliefs, you are not going to get away with that. The person will not follow your commands at all. In fact, this can backfire as well.

ANALOG MARKING

Downward inflection of the voice to impress subconscious mind is also called analog marking the part of sentence to the subconscious mind.

You can do it in many other ways also. For example, if you are a motivational speaker, you can raise the voice at the particular embedded command rather than downwardly inflecting it.

You can also put a pause around it. For example, "And the prince said to princess, "My Dear, You can….. relax now…""

Other way is through the hand gestures. You would have noticed that many people use their hands to make a point. Sometimes when they are aggressive they will beat a table, or thump their chests etc. This makes those words stand out in the sentence and is another sort of marking.

You can use the same technique. For example, when you say 'relax now' in above dialogue, just move your hand slowly as if you are underlining something. I call this technique – underlining the content to the subconscious mind.

Milton Erickson could not underline the embedded commands with his hands due to his disability. So, he would mark the embedded commands by moving his upper body from side to side.

You can embed commands in multiple ways. The subconscious mind is many times more alert than what we think it to be.

CHAPTER 18
HYPNOTIC LANGUAGE PATTERNS

Hypnotic Language Patterns are derived from the study of Milton H. Erickson's work. Milton was using these artfully vague language patterns unconsciously and achieving remarkable results.

Richard Bandler and John Grinder studied his works and documented the patterns he was using. They named it as The Milton Model.

Then they tried these patterns themselves and achieved remarkable results. These patterns are designed to make the conscious mind unconscious and directly influence the subconscious mind of the person.

Hence this is a very powerful tool in an Influencer's kit. These patterns are being used in sales, negotiation, motivational speeches and hypnotherapy. They form the basis of Ericksonian Hypnosis.

Let us go through these patterns now. Do not expect to master this chapter in one reading. Each pattern is unique and they need to be practiced for several days.

My suggestion is to set a regular time for practice. Then select two or three patterns and write as long as you can. The more you practice the better you become.

THE MILTON MODEL

Mind Reading

Claiming to know someone's thoughts or feelings without specifying how you got to know that information.

Examples:

"I know that you are the kind of person who want to grow his influencing skills."

"I know you are finding this book helpful in improving your persuasion skills."

"You must be feeling like attending an NLP training to take your persuasion skills to the next level."

Lost Performative

A value judgement is made without specifying who has made the judgement.

Examples:

"Influencing is a great art."

"Influencing is easy once you have right kind of training."

"Everyone is playing the influencing game whole life."

Cause-Effect

Implying that a particular action causes a specific reaction or response. This pattern is characterized by words such as: because, if/then, makes, drives, compels, causes.

Examples:

"Attending NLP program will take your influencing skills to the next level."

"Influencing is good because it creates win-win situations."

"You must learn to influence others because only then you will be able to go to the next level."

Complex Equivalence

Suggests that one action, experience or behavior means something another without explanation or proof.

Examples:

"Reading this book means that you are interested in influencing others."

"You have come so far in this book, that means you have already learned lot of wonderful stuff."

"The fact that you are reading this line means that you are finding Milton Model interesting."

Presupposition

Something unstated has to be assumed to be true for the statement to be understood.

They are of two types:

Temporal presuppositions

Related to time. These are characterized by words like when, after, during, before, while.

Examples:

When you complete this book, you will want to join us in a live event to learn more.

After you join our live event, your influencing skills will be at an entirely different level.

Ordinal presuppositions

Give sequence to the listener's experience by using numbers or positions.

Examples:

"First we will go through these language patterns and then we will take up another interesting topic."

"Let us see who joins our live event first."

Universal Quantifier

This pattern is used as if implying there is no exception to the experience stated.

Examples:

"Everyone has the experience of going into trance."

"Anyone can learn the art and science of influencing."

Modal Operators or Necessity or Probability

Modal operators of necessity

These patterns suggest that something is required or not required to happen. You can generate this pattern by using words such as: must, mustn't, should, shouldn't, need to, have to etc.

Examples:

"You needn't even bother to think about attend the transformational live event with Naresh."

Modal operators of probability

Modal operators of probability include words such as: can, can't, possible, impossible, will, won't, may, may not.

Examples:

"You can easily notice how much confident you have already started feeling about yourself."

Simple Deletion

Information is left out of the statement.

Examples:

"You are feeling confident."

"You are doing great."

Nominalization

A process has been turned into a thing. That is verbs are turned into nouns.

Examples: Nominalizations are in italics.

"You can have great influence in your circle and out of it."

"By the end of this book you will have total confidence in the power of influence that you possess"

Unspecified Verb.

Action is implied, without describing how the action has occurred or will occur.

Examples:

"You can imagine how your influencing skills will be much better."

"People with influence are running the world."

Comparative Deletion (Unspecified Comparison).

A comparison is made but it is not clear as to who or what is being compared to.

Examples:

"After reading this book, you will be far more influential" (More influential? Than whom?)

"Our NLP and Influencing trainings are better" (Better than what? Or better than whom?)

Lack of referential Index

 The subject (who) of the statement is unspecified.

Examples:

"People can change become influenced more easily than they think." (Here term people does not specify who specifically is referred to)

"One can very soon feel the effects of using NLP regularly."

Tag question

A question added at the end of a statement. This pattern is designed to increase compliance.

Examples:

"As you read these patterns, your become more and more confident in your influencing capabilities, isn't it?"

Pacing current experience

You pace other person's internal or external sensory experience. This is also known as "yes sets" principle. After pacing you can plant your suggestion.

Examples:

"You are reading this book …."

"and going through these words…"

"reading sentence after sentence."

"That means you are enjoying the powerful content of this book". (Suggestion)

Double bind.

Illusion of choice. This means the choice is given for how but not for the underlying motive. One example is the salesperson asking – "Are you going to pay by cash or card?". There is clear choice seems to given in the sentence. However, it is superficial choice. The salesperson wants you to pay for the item.

Examples:

"Would you like to attend our live event before finishing this book or after?"

"Do you want to sit in this chair, or the other one to go into trance?"

"You want to be hypnotized in 30 seconds or less than 30 seconds?"

Embedded commands

A command forms part of a larger sentence. This command is delivered with different tonality with downward inflection of the voice.

Examples: Embedded commands are marked in italics.

"We are not *saying that change is easy*."

"It's good that you have *decided to learn NLP* and become a better person."

Conversational postulate

A "rhetorical question" is asked with intention of getting something done. If taken literally, would require a response or action. These may also include Embedded Commands.

Examples:

"Can you give me a glass of water?"

"Could you please finish this work by end of the day?"

Extended quote

A succession of quotes designed to create mild confusion in the listener, increase suggestibility and compliance, and embed process instructions or commands.

Examples:

Some time ago I was training in Bangalore conducted by Naresh Kumar, and one of the participants said, "You know I have been to many trainings and yours is the most transformational one…. Even my wife told me, 'When you go to these trainings you seem so fresh and so relaxed. Even the children are saying, "Dad has transformed so much by going to these amazing trainings… we don't know what the trainer does in the workshop, but whatever it is, it is amazing" '

Selectional Restriction Violation

Attributing intelligence or feelings to inanimate objects.

Examples:

"The symptom is saying, it is time to heal."

"This chair can feel proud you know."

"This room will be witness to all the amazing transformations that are happening here."

Ambiguity

Words and statements with more than one meaning. This means that there will be several deep structures for the same structure. This will put the person in mild confusion, triggering trans-derivational search.

Phonological Ambiguity

Words/phrases written differently, but sounding same.

Examples:

"Your unconscious"/" You're unconscious"

"by now"/" buy now"

"reduce the waste"/" reduce the waist"

apart/a part, I/eye, heel/heal, know/no, sea/see, write/right, not/knot, hole/whole

Syntactic Ambiguity

Syntactic function of the word of phrase cannot easily be determined from the utterance. Or confusing syntax.

Examples:

"Hypnotizing hypnotists can be tricky."

"Investigating FBI agents can be dangerous."

"Speaking to you as a person determined to change."

Scope Ambiguity

Scope/context is not clear.

Examples:

"The disturbing thoughts and feelings." (are the feelings also disturbing?)

"The long days and night." (are the nights also long?)

Punctuation Ambiguity

Well-formed sentences joined by a word or phrase to create and ill-formed sentence.

Examples:

"I like your watch your breathing begins to slow down."

"You can learn how to relax each muscle in your body."

"I like your smile that the hard times are gone and future is bright."

Utilization

Pacing internal/external experiences of the subject. Whatever happens can be utilized as part of the process.

Examples:

"All the external noises will help you focus on my voice"

"You are sitting here, listening to me and probably wondering about what is going to happen"

"That's right."

Factive (Awareness) Predicates

Presupposing truth by the use of words like: realize, know, become aware of, understand.

Examples:

"Have you noticed that your body has begun to relax naturally."

"As you become aware of your breathing, you start to feel more comfortable."

Commentary adjectives and adverbs

Words that make the listener inclined to accept the quality of everything that follows, such as: kindly, usefully, surprisingly.

Examples:

"Interestingly, your unconscious is a very intelligent system."

"Clearly, you are looking very relaxed now."

How to use the Milton Model Language Patterns

Milton Model language patterns are very powerful and effective. You can start using them during your normal day-to-day conversations first. When you use the patterns with people, they usually go into a state of mild confusion. However, very often you will find them enjoying the conversation. The reason is that just using these patterns for few minutes puts people in light trance. They don't want the trance to be broken. They will be fully engrossed in your artfully vague language.

Next time you read a newspaper, or hear a top politician's speech, just listen carefully and keep these patterns at the back of your mind. You will often find them that these politicians are using these patterns all the time.

Take a challenge to detect as many patterns as you can. The more you practice the better you become.

The easiest way is to start with <u>Metaphor</u> approach. You can start telling stories to children or someone who are easy to practice with. And while you are telling stories, use as many patterns from this chapter, and enjoy watching them enjoying all that you have to say fully engrossed and totally in love with what you have to say.

CHAPTER 19
META-MODEL

Meta-Model is language model derived from Virginia Satir's work. Meta-Model is where the NLP started. It was the first model of NLP. Virginia Satir was a family therapist and was getting great results in family therapy just as Ericskson was getting good results in his work. However, her linguistic approach was completely opposite to Milton Ericson. While Ericksonian Hypnosis uses artfully vague language for change work, Virginia's approach was to use specific language to create change. She would ask questions after questions in order to get clarity from the client and in the process the client would also get clarity for himself. Due to this reason, Meta-Model is also called the first practical model for Life Coaching.

To summarize the Milton Model creates confusion by using three techniques – Deletion, Distortion, Generalization. However, the meta-model worked by recovering what is deleted and mending what is distorted and breaking the non-resourceful generalizations. Here are the questions of Meta-Model, along with the corresponding Milton Model questions.

DELETIONS

Simple Deletion

Information is left out of the statement.

Example: I am stuck.

Question: How do you know you are stuck?

This question will make the person to scan his present situation and list down things which are making him stuck. Once he does that, you have specific things to work with.

Unspecified Referential Index.

The subject of the statement is unspecified.

Example: They just don't help our team.

Question: Who specifically don't help your team?

Again, the answer will give you more concrete information to work with. Knowledge about other person is power in the world of influence.

Comparative Deletion (Unspecified Comparison)

A comparison is made but it is not clear as to who or what is being compared to.

Example: Their team is better.

Question: Better than whom?

or

Better than what?

Unspecified Verb

Agent of an action is unclear.

Example: They are creating problems for our team.

Question: Who/how/what problems specifically? How do you know they are creating problems for you?

Nominalization

A process or adjective has been turned into a thing.

Example: My reputation is in trouble.

Question: What about the way in which you relating is troubling you?

The nominalizations are easy to slip away. The way to work with them is to convert them back into processes or adjectives.

DISTORTIONS

Mind Reading

The speaker claims to know or acts as if he knows, what is going on in other person's mind or their feeling/beliefs.

Example: They will feel angry when I go there.

Question: How do you know?

Lost performative

A value judgement is made without stating who has made the judgement.

Example: One should take care of others' interests before his interests.

Question: As per whom? Or according to whom?

Cause-Effect

A particular action is taken to cause a specific response of reaction.

Hint: Listen to words like because, if/then, causes, makes, drives, compels etc.

Example: The way she talks to me drives me crazy.

Question: How specifically her talking to you drives you crazy?

Complex Equivalence

One action, experience or behavior is taken to mean another without explanation or proof

Hint: Listen for – means, therefore, implies.

Example: His trip was so brief, he must have lost the deal.

Question: How does a short trip mean that he has lost the deal? Or (counter example) Have you ever had a short trip and yet cracked a deal?

Presupposition.

An assumption or assumptions (unstated in the sentence), taken to be present or true for the sentence to be understood.

Example: When are you going to start to show your affection?

Question: How do you know I am not showing affection?

GENERALIZATIONS

Universal Quantifiers

Implying there is no exception to the experience stated.

Hint: Listen for words like: always. Never, ever, all, No one, everyone, everything, nothing etc.

Example: No one loves me

Question: (Exaggerate) What? Always? Not even you? Or

(Counter example): You said your dog jumps with joy when you go home. Doesn't that mean he loves you?

Modal Operators or Necessity or Probability.

Example: I can't get started in the morning.

Question:

What would happen if you could get started?

What stops you from getting started in the morning?

CHAPTER 20
METAPHORS

Many years ago, I remember one of my friends coming for advice to me. She described how hard her life is, how she is facing hardships in life. She kept on going on and on. And how bad her life has become.

When she was done with her talk, I said to her," You see, life is not a *bed of roses*. It is neither good nor bad. Life is what it is. It is different for everyone. You have to make most out of it. If the destiny hands you a *lemon*, you cannot change it, but you can make a *lemonade* out of it"

And that changed her state. She went into a thoughtful mode. And then she said, "I think you are right, I have to make most out of my life, even though it is not a *bed of roses.*"

It was a tremendous shift from negative to thoughtful mode.

In the above instance, I compared the life to a *"bed of roses"*. This is called metaphor. In the same sense, the lack of sophistication in life are compared to *lemon* and the process of making best out of the circumstances is compared to *making a lemonade.*

Metaphor means when we are describing one concept in terms of another concept. This is very effective tool in reframing or explaining complex concepts in simple way.

When I was young, one day I looked at a big glass marble. It was a soft, shining green color marble with lot of air bubbles of all sizes, inside it. Somehow it seemed to resemble the solar system or other universe's images I had seen in my science book. I was amazed at the similarity. Just like there is a sun at the center surrounded by nine planets of all sizes, there was a bubble which was at the center and there were many big and small bubbles around it.

And surprisingly when I later looked at the images in the book they looked more interesting and engaging.

This is metaphor in action.

Metaphors are used in learning from day one. For example, our teachers used to tell that earth is like an orange. And that made it simpler to imagine earth.

"Sun is a giant ball of fire", was another common metaphor we heard about.

A metaphor can be as simple as a single word like "orange" or a phrase like "ball of fire". At more complex level metaphor can also be a story with a message.

WHY METAPHORS ARE SO POWERFUL

Metaphor is the language of subconscious mind. The subconscious mind stores the complex information in terms of simple metaphors.

For example, for some people the life feels like a *pleasant journey* and other find it like *climbing a steep hill.* Some people have hard times due to *teething problems* in the new project.

All the *italicized* words or phrases are examples of metaphors.

When we are talking to someone in the language or metaphors, we are stimulating a phenomenon called trans-derivational search (TDS).

TDS means that to make sense of what is said, the listener has to go into an altered state and find the answer from the subconscious part of the mind. And when it happens the person is highly suggestible and prone to influence.

To answer your metaphor the person very often has to come up with his own metaphoric answer. That means you are controlling not only what goes inside someone's mind as well as the direction of the conversation.

STORY TELLING

Story telling comes under metaphors. Stories are a powerful tool of influence. That is the reason that you will find all great influencers can keep the audience engaged for hours with lot of stories.

And with practice they gather a number of stories over a period of time.

You must keep a log of various stories you can tell in one-on-one conversations or in presentations.

WHERE TO FIND THE STORIES FROM

Here are four sources of stories for you.

The most effective stories are from your real life. Keep noting down all the instances which you can use in your conversations or presentations.

The second-best source is what happened to the others. For this you have to be a good listener. This is where many of your stories will come from if you are listening to your friends or the people who meet by chance in parties or trains.

The third best source is books and magazines. Most of your stories are going to come from these sources.

The fourth one is made up stories. Not all stories have to really happen in your life. If it is required feel free to make up story on the fly.

METAPHORS/STORIES ARE EVERYWHERE

Stories are everywhere around us. We are living in a world full of stories. Sometimes we do not realize a story when it is presented to us.

For example, you go to buy a car, the car salesman is selling you story about how your life will change once you have his car.

A property salesman is trying to sell you the story of a beautiful life in the house that they are showing.

All advertisements are also selling you stories.

All newspapers and TV News Channels are presenting you stories only.

STORIES FOR ELICITING DESIRED STATES

Stories can also be used to elicit specific states in audience. The way you structure the stories also matters a lot. You can either tell three separate stories to elicit three different states in audience. Or you can tell one single story with a sequence of events where all three states come one after other in a sequence.

While telling stories you can embed suggestions in the stories by using Milton Model's embedding quote pattern.

All that you have to quote a character and say like – then Tom said to me, "You have to feel motivated to change. You have to welcome the change and be awesome at what you do."

NESTED LOOPS

Nested loop a clever way of embedding suggestions in a series of stories. It is based upon the fact that the mind wants to close a loop i.e. if you start a conversation and abruptly switch to another conversation, the listener's mind may go restless as the first conversation was not concluded.

You can start a story and then add some embedded suggestions at appropriate stage. However before completing story you start another story and put some more embedded commands. You keep doing this to 3-5 levels.

This way you will have multiple stories which you started but moved on to the next story without ending it. This will put the listener in mild trance. The listener will be very suggestible or prone to influence.

Then you close the stories one by one in reverse way. That means you close the fifth story, followed by fourth, third, second and ultimately the first story.

At every stage, you can embed relevant commands.

EXERCISE

Combine Nested Loops with Milton Model and speak from the depth of your belly and you have a powerful weapon capable of influencing people.

For this exercise, select an outcome for someone. In the beginning, it helps to have a relatively simple positive outcome, e.g. relaxation. Come up with three real or made up stories which you can use in this context.

Decide on the embedded commands for relaxation.

Now start telling first story and in the middle start second story. While you are telling the second story, start the third story. At appropriate place in the third story embed the commands you decided.

It is easier to say something like, and then so-and-so said," You can be relaxed, and feel wonderful. As you relax notice your body going limp and find a part of body which has already relaxed. Now take that relaxation and spread throughout your body and notice how your mind relaxes with your body, isn't it?... "and then continue with the story.

After finishing story #3, go ahead and close story #2 and then story#1. You can embed commands at any of the steps mentioned, e.g. before closing story#2 or story#1.

CHAPTER 21
THE POWER OF SILENCE

One day the Buddha silently held up a white flower before his disciples. He did not utter even a single word. As he was sitting there, one disciple got powerful insight and smiled at Buddha. Buddha understood the transformation and smiled back. This was the famous "Flower Sermon" and is cited very often in Buddhism and Zen.

Buddha used the power of silence to convey things which could not be conveyed through words.

This may be an extreme example of using silence as a weapon of influence. However, you will often find highly influential people who speak very less, but when they speak the whole group listens.

Silence puts you in a position of strength, a position of power. By staying silent and maintaining confident yet eye contact, you are sending subtle signals which convey that you're in control of your reactions, you're in control of your emotions and you're in control of the situation. People look at you as a person who probably has lot of stuff in his head and will speak the right thing when the right time comes.

When people want to influence others, they focus more on what to say and how to say it. Talking is most important tool in influence, but only when you have the content and clarity of thought. Without clarity of thought it can have reverse effect.

In fact, no amount of influence tools can help you, if your thought process is not clear.

Mark Twain said, "It is better to let others think you a fool than to open your mouth and remove all doubt."

Try this in the next conversation that you have. Say as little as possible and get them to do nearly all the talking.

Before we go further, I would like to tell you that silent may not be appropriate in many situations. If you're silent at a conversational setting where you're trying to influence somebody to change a belief, take a certain course of action, make a certain deal etc., often silence is the worst thing to do. You do need to say things, you do need to stimulate emotions, and get your point across.

BRIEF PAUSES

One of the ways to use the power of silence is by inserting deliberate pauses while you speak. Give yourself few extra seconds before you respond to the other person.

While you are on pause, the other person's anticipation will build up. And that will make them more prone to be influenced. They will be more respectful to what is coming, as subconsciously they will believe that you have used the pause to think through what you are going to tell and hence it is more important and meaningful.

LEVERAGING THE POWER OF SILENCE IN PUBLIC SPEECHES

Most good speakers, would energetically come on the stage and immediately begin talking and engage the audience with their enthusiasm, energy, jokes etc.

On the other hand, bad speakers would shuffle onstage and also begin talking immediately. The difference is that they will do it less energetically and in a more withdrawn way.

However, an extremely powerful way to immediately capture the audience's attention, is to walk on stage calmly, look around at the audience and just maintain your silence. Hold your silence, just until it becomes uncomfortable.

When you do this, you will be sending a lot of powerful messages at subconscious level. It is like, you're saying you're in control of yourself and your responses. That you're so completely comfortable and justified and assured in your own presence that you do not need to speak to justify yourself being there.

You will notice that your silence will lead the audience into silence.

If there is noise, as it happens after breaks or starting of day, you will notice that first people will stop talking among themselves. Then there may be confusion and little bit of murmur. Then at some point front rows people would start looking eagerly at you. This behavior will cascade to middle and last rows. And very soon you will have almost everyone's attention.

At this point, most of them would have lowered their guards and be far more receptive to your content. A mediocre content will produce good results in this situation. A good content will produce excellent result and excellent content will produce stellar outcome for the audience and you. And people will remember you weeks, months or even years after your presentation. Silence as an effective influence tool can be exceedingly powerful.

Maintain the silence only until it becomes uncomfortable and then wait just one more second before talking.

SILENCE AND RELATIONSHIPS

On personal level, if you think back to spending time with someone you love, perhaps your spouse or your family, you'll realize that silence is actually a part of your relationship. You can be silent in each other's presence without it being hostile or uncomfortable.

HOW OFTEN TO USE SILENCE?

Silence as a tool should be used a limited amount. It's like when you learn a really powerful quote. It will blow people away when you use it once in a conversation or in one speech. This will act as an instant re-frame and really orient the discussion towards where you want to take it.

However, people will get annoyed if you use it several times every day, day after day.

You want use silence to build suspense, to build mystery, to build curiosity and to put the pressure on the other people.

CHAPTER 22
BODY LANGUAGE FOR INFLUENCE

Your body language is a powerful influence tool.

Now, books and books and books have been written on body language. Telling you this gesture means that, that gesture means this, crossing the arms means defensive, scratching the nose means lying, open posture means confident, this, that or the other.

And after reading a book on body language, you may or may not remember a lot of stuff. Also, many times you would wish you had a handy manual or mobile app which you could refer to during the conversation as you keep forgetting what does a particular posture mean.

Let me make it simple for you so that you will have a general sense of what a person's body language may mean.

First of all, body language is a process through with we communicate with others. When the primitive man had no language skills, they used the body language to communicate. And this process is more or less the same as it was that time. We have just added language and vocabulary to our communication. Not much has changed with respect to how we communicated through our body language.

To understand this, consider how do mammals without language skill communicated. Let us say how do mammals like Dogs or wild animals communicate through their bodies, when they are about to fight. If you recall then it is fine and continue reading, else stop reading and go to the Internet and find some animal videos.

Before a fight the weaker or unconfident animals, will depict defensive body language. The survival instincts in them, will try to protect his vulnerable parts like his neck, stomach and his groin. Many times, you will see that the weaker animal will sit down on the ground. Or it will turn away from the strong animal often with head down and/or tail between its legs. That is the body of weak animal will always shrink.

On the other hand, the stronger animal will expand his body, expose his neck, stomach and groin (e.g. monkeys) to show its strength. It is like saying, that he is not afraid of anyone. He is sure about his strength and is in control.

The same logic applies to humans also. We are also mammals and more important have been through this conditioning for millions of years.

Now, this is why things like crossing your arms, putting your hand on your face, scratching your nose, are often thought of as signs of deceptiveness or defensiveness. Because you are invariably covering the vulnerable areas (neck, stomach and groin etc.) of your bodies.

Whereas when you're confident, you always open up those areas. This is seen in sports all the time. The winners for example, will have a body language which communicate the feeling of being invincible. For example, their chin will be up (uncovering neck), their arms will be stretched outwards and above their head (uncovering neck, chest and stomach), their chest will be outwards (uncovering chest and stomach). On the other hand, the losers will depict shrinking body language with head down, shoulders dropped and walking at slower pace. They may be crossing their arms for say scratching their nose. Scratching nose is a very common gesture when people feel vulnerable. Try to remember the last time you have seen a winner scratching his nose immediately after winning.

Now when you understand the underlying concept, you will not have to remember what I mentioned in the parenthesis. I can make this stuff up on the fly by just knowing the logic of why these things happen. Just understand – open body language means confident and in control. Closed body language means – withdrawing, fearful and out of control.

The same thing happens during the conversations. The person with weak point will feel threatened. And the millions of years of training will come into picture and his body language will become closed.

On the other hand, a person has no reason to feel threatened, will depict open body language.

That is the reason that the influential people have open body language. They are very sure of what they are saying. They have the conviction of what they do.

Rather than teaching you this gesture means this, that gesture means that, I think it's far more powerful for you to come to an understanding of the language of the body.

You can use this fact while you are influencing others. Regardless of how you are feeling inside, always adopt an open body language during your conversations.

The mind and body are one system. You change what is happening in one of them and you will automatically change the other. So invariably you will start automatically feeling in control and confident.

Exercise: Mind Body Connection

1.   Think about a conversation which is not comfortable, a conversation where you are on backfoot. For example, status update to your nagging boss or something equivalent. Think about this for couple of minutes.

2.   Now notice what happens to your body. What kind of body language you are exhibiting. Is it open or closed? Mostly it will be closed only, unless your way of handling this situation is to act being confident in front of your boss by displaying open body language.

3.   Now stretch your arms above your head, take a deep breath fill up your lungs, look up towards the roof, smile, grin and say – "To hell with him". And shake your body.

4.   Drop your arms and as you are sitting notice how are you feeling and how is your body language now.

BODY LANGUAGE AND SILENCE

And when you're not speaking, when you're silent, the way you hold yourself becomes more and more important.

If you're silent with a shrinking posture, with your arms folded and/or, maybe your hand over your mouth, it can make you seem quite withdrawn, quite defensive.

However, if you're silent with an open posture, with hand perhaps on the face to indicate thinking, but open with your stomach and neck while exposed, perhaps raised eyebrows to indicate curiosity, and firm yet calm and reassuring eye contact with the people you're speaking to it's encouraging them to keep speaking. It puts the ball in their court and the pressure on them.

CHAPTER 23
ART OF FRAME CONTROL

In any conversation, the person who controls the frame controls is the one who has the highest influence.

Frame control is like a controlling a spotlight. Through the art of frame control you can control which part of the conversation to put the spotlight on.

Frame control in few words means to control the determine in which direction the conversation is going to go. In other way leading the discussion and ultimately the outcome of the discussion.

An entire book can be written on the art of frame control. However, that will complicate the things, isn't it?

So, let me simplify the whole process.

The art of frame control is also called reframing.

WHAT IS REFRAMING?

Reframing is a method of using language to influence over someone's thoughts. It is one of the most powerful tools in influence. And it should be used carefully. Most of the bad reputation of NLP comes from misuse of reframing.

Reframing is all about changing the way you perceive an event. This change of perception changes the meaning and hence response and behavior as well.

WHAT IS A FRAME?

The frame is the way someone is viewing or perceiving an event. Have you ever experienced a situation where you are with a friend and something unexpected happens? For example, a fight breaks out at a traffic signal. And when you discuss later on, both of you have different understanding of who was right and who was wrong. One for example may be sympathizing with the person whose car got damaged. And the other might be feeling that since he was violating the traffic rules, he knew the risk he was taking. And that some people learn in hard ways.

This is happening because both of you are viewing the even from different points of views or frames. By the way, have you considered that one can think of the phrase 'point of view', to be like a 'view-point'. They both sound to mean something similar, on in the external eyes and other in the eye of the inner mind. A view point determines what is captured in a frame and what is left out. So, when people have different points of view, they are actually looking at problem from different inner view points and that means with different frames.

RICHER FRAME = MORE INFLUENCE

A great way to increase your influence is to consider other person's point of view. Look at the situation from his frame. What is he including in the frame and what is he leaving out. And if his frame is wider or have finer details, you can enrich your frame with missing details and thus make your frame much more inclusive and richer. This strengthens your frame. Earlier you had ten points and other person had five points. Now you have fifteen points. It is like capturing a scenery in panoramic view. You can then do wonders with this information.

Shakespeare said, "There is nothing good or bad only thinking makes it so."

I'd say there is nothing good or bad only framing makes it so.

The frame that you put around a situation, an event or a problem, is what makes it real and it determines the emotions you have about it and how you interact with it.

PRE-FRAMING

There are multiple ways you can control the direction of a conversation.

If you happen to be the one who is starting the conversation or meeting, you can do something called pre-framing.

Pre-framing means setting the agenda or tone of the conversation. As the people agree to the agenda, you will be invoking the principle of commitment and consistency. That means you will have a great edge. The moment the conversation starts going in other direction, you can interrupt and tell people that the new topic can be discussed in another meeting.

So, you will have great control over the direction and outcome of the meeting.

TYPES OF FRAMES

To be good at frame control, the first step is to learn various types of frames. NLP has beautifully categorized various types of frames. Below is simplified version of these frames:

Outcome Frame

An outcome frame provides a focus for what you want to achieve. Here the focus is on the end result. For example, an outcome could be to have a well-balanced life. Or in professional setting the outcome could be to increase the productivity of the engineering staff by 10% in the coming quarter.

Ecology Frame

Ecology frame is meant to evaluate the effects of what you are doing or going to do. For example, if you want to increase the production of your factory by 10% then it is going to have some good and bad side effects also. A good side effect could be that you and your staff get higher bonus this year. And a bad side effect could be that the staff may burn out or they may be missing out on personal life.

Whenever you set an outcome in outcome frame, change this to ecology frame to find out what kind of side effects is this outcome going to produce and whether this outcome is worth having or not.

Evidence Frame

When you are working towards your outcome, you need to have some sort of evidence to validate two things:

1. You are on track

2. You have arrived at/achieved the outcome

The first point is achieved by setting relevant milestones.

A milestone is a smaller goal which helps you to achieve a bigger goal. For example, if you want to have a new house in three, the milestones could be to finalize on a land within one month, arrange loan and start work by the end of second month, and complete the work by third month. This is a very simple example of milestone and some aspects of it may not seem practical to you, however the point is to get the point.

Now, going with this example, if by the end of the first month you have not finalized the land, then you are not likely to have the house by the end of three months. Milestones keep a tab on our progress.

The second type of evidence you need is when you have achieved the goal. While setting the outcome, you can specify that by the end of the third month you should move into your new house. This will be your evidence for goal completion.

As if Frame

This frame has many applications and is based on acting 'as if' a desired state or outcome has been achieved.

• For an outcome, act as if you have already achieved your outcome. Live your dreams now and allow reality to catch up!

• When negotiating, you can use 'as if' frame to explore other possibilities. For example, you can say, "Fine! Let us assume that I agree to what you are proposing. What would you do for me and what would happen next."

• For backward planning your projects. For example, you may act 'as if' your project is complete in next 3 months. Then brainstorm what will be the second last step to achieve this. And once you have finalized the second last step, again act 'as if' the second last step is achieved and now brainstorm what has to happen for the second last step to be achieved… this way you will arrive at third last step and so on.

- If someone is missing from a meeting, you may say, "Let us act as if Michael is present… and let us proceed accordingly".

Backtrack Frame

This frame can be used to check agreement and understanding during and at the conclusion of a conversation.

During the conversation, keep noting things down either mentally or on a paper that the person said. Note down the keywords and key phrases. At the end check with the person whether your understanding is right or not. When you are doing this, it is called backtrack frame.

We all filter information differently and may come to significantly different conclusions. Backtracking is a way to ensure everyone has the same understanding of what was discussed and decided.

Feedback Versus Failure Frame

This frame is based upon following NLP presupposition:

There is no failure only feedback.

Often when things do not go well, people consider this as their failure and they get into self-critical mode. Once you keep this presupposition in mind that there is no failure and only feedback, then it opens up the channels for learning. You can ask what things we can learn from what has happened. And what can we do to prevent from repeating this in the future.

Blame Frame

This is a dangerous frame. As the name suggests, it is when people are blaming each other and/or the circumstances for their conditions and results. The idea of putting this here is to be aware of this frame when it happens. When this happens, and this will happen pretty regularly, bring them back to one of the helpful frames we mentioned above.

FRAME CONTROL FOR BEGINNERS

Now how to use this information as a beginner. There are many ways of frame control. The most effective is by directing people to switch into an appropriate frame.

For example, when people are in blaming frame, you can ask them what do they want instead? And this will immediately put them into outcome frame.

And when people are cursing each other or someone else for their failures, just tell, "Whatever has happened has happened. What are few things we can learn from this whole incident so that we can take better care of such situations in future?"

This will guide people into feedback vs failure frame.

When everyone seems confused and lost, just tell, "let us list down what we want to achieve." And that will put everyone in outcome frame. And when they have specified the outcome, just tell, "Let us determine our milestones." This will put people in evidence frame.

Similarly, as per situation you can use ecology and "as if" frames as well.

Now frame control or reframing is a vast topic and entire workshops have been run alone on this topic. For the beginners, what I have described till now is enough to practice.

CHAPTER 24
GO THERE FIRST

In this, chapter we are going to discuss a tool called "go there first". The idea behind this is, if you want somebody to feel a certain way, i.e. in other words, to enter a certain state of mind – you have to enter that certain state of mind yourself beforehand.

As explained earlier, your state of being affects your body language, your delivery, the way you think and the words you say.

Imagine a time in your recent past when you were a little annoyed about something, maybe a little angry, and then imagine another time when you were happy, relaxed, feeling good. And notice how the way you communicated in those two instances were completely and 110% different.

People pick up on this. Not always consciously but always subconsciously. And this subconscious level communication determines how you come across. This has a huge impact on the effects of your communication.

Now the reason that this principle works is because of a phenomenon called mirror neurons. When you are in rapport with someone, then there are certain neurons in both of your brains which will mirror each other. That is the reason that when a one of you shifts his position the other person also shifts his position. And this happens at emotional level as well.

Hence first step is to be able to manage your own state of mind. You need to be able to control what state of mind you go into during a particular interaction.

Now, this works when you're making somebody feel happy, getting rapport with somebody else, because rapport after all is actually just a feeling, isn't it? It's a feeling of liking, it's a feeling of trust and it's a feeling of connection. If you want somebody to feel those things towards you, you naturally want to feel those things towards them as well, so that through your body language and through your sub-communications, you can project that and they will respond to it.

Another key reason why we go there first is because it allows you to deal with people with what therapists call, "An unconditional positive regard." Now, in a persuasion and influence setting, this gives you an amazingly massive upper hand, this unconditional positive regard. Looking at somebody in such a way that no matter how they behave, no matter who they are, no matter what they do, you still regard them positively.

You can still evaluate them, this doesn't mean you can't make evaluations on whether they'd be suitable for certain business decisions or certain personal decisions, you can still be sensible and logical in that way, however this unconditional positive regard puts you in a very strong position of power. Because if you hold somebody in unconditional – that's the key word, unconditional – positive regard, then even if they do something unethical or annoying or something that would normally get you a bit annoyed and make you think, "Oh no, I was wrong to like this person," they no longer have that emotional power over you.

When you regard somebody unconditionally, that means your feelings about them are entirely your decision. However, if you're waiting to base your emotional responses on somebody, depending on how they react and how they behave and what they say and what they do, then they own you emotionally. And if you dislike somebody, don't they have complete control over your emotions? Aren't they in the unique and powerful position of being able to make you enter a powerful emotional state, albeit a negative one, merely by their presence and by their natural behavior?

However, if you hold these people in unconditional positive regard or, sometimes a bit easier, unconditional neutral regard, they are just there. It's not disdain or ignorance, it's unconditional regard. Your regard for them is unconditional. However, you're still able to make logical evaluations, then you're fine.

Now, evaluations aren't judgments. Judgments are, "I like this person, I don't like this person, they're a good person, they're a bad person." Evaluations are, "Yeah, I probably don't want to go approaching this 6'9" person with a machete on the street and ask him for directions," that's an evaluation, it's not a judgment.

Now, how does this relate to go there first?

In order to be able to go there first, you need to be able to completely control your emotional state in any given interaction. If you want to say, "Right, I want to make this person feel calm and relaxed," you need to immediately be able to feel calm and relaxed yourself. If they emotionally control you, if you dislike them or if you're in such a state of mind that you're going along with their emotional state of being, then you won't be able to fully enter that state of calm relaxation and you won't be able to speak from that position congruently or powerfully and help them enter that state of mind as well.

Hopefully you can understand this.

Where this puts you therefore is in a uniquely powerful position because you hold them in unconditional regard, and you realize the power of go there first, so if you want them to enter a particular state of mind, you merely need to enter it yourself.

How do you do that? It's really quite simple. You see, throughout your life, you will have had in your life every single emotional reference experience you need. That is to say, there are times in your life where you've felt happy. There are times in your life where you've felt excited. There are times in your life where you've felt relaxed. And there are times in your life where you've felt calm.

I'm sure you can remember examples of all these times right now. Think about a time right now that you felt calm and relaxed. It doesn't have to be the calmest and relaxed you've ever felt, it just needs to be a nice sort of calm and relaxed time.

Now as you're thinking about that time, I want you to really focus, not so much on the memory itself, but on that feeling. And as you're focusing on that feeling, I want you to imagine as if that feeling had a color. Now as you randomly ascribe a color to that feeling, whatever color that feeling seems to be, there's no right or wrong answer, imagine that that color and that feeling has a location in your body. And when you've identified the location of that feeling and that color, I simply want you to imagine it becoming brighter, more powerful, more intense and spreading from that location all over your body, moving this happy, calm feeling and spreading it all over.

As you do that, I'm sure you're beginning to realize that you really can have control over your feelings. All you need to do is go back into your unlimited store of references and memories, choose the appropriate feeling for the situation, and imagine yourself immersing yourself in that feeling, and allowing that feeling to spread to every inch of your body.

As you do that, you'll get better and better, and the more you practice, the quicker, easier and the more powerful it will become.

When you first start doing it in a normal conversation, you may feel a bit odd to sort of pause, go inside your mind and think about a good feeling, and it may take thirty seconds. With practice, you will be able to enter into any state by just thinking about it.

The more you practice, the better you're going to get at this.

THE MAGNETIC STRATEGY

The magnetic strategy, as I call it, is an effective technique to lead people into the states that you want. And this magnetic strategy has three steps. It is mainly used to change the state of the other person.

Step 1:

First of all, you identify what state of mind they're in now and what state of mind you would like them to be in. So, let's say they were in an anxious state of mind but you want to move them into a calm state of mind. That's step one.

Step 2:

Step two, is gain rapport by entering into their state of mind. So, you temporarily enter into an anxious state of mind by remembering a time when you were anxious. However, it doesn't have to be a state of panic; it's just a minor, tiny, tiny, tiny sample of that state. Like a vaccination, it's a tiny, tiny, tiny sample of an illness to allow you to build up and be stronger and resist it. This will help you enter into their world and communicate with them at their level in the world they're in, in the reality in which they're in. So that's step two, temporarily enter their state of mind.

Step 3:

And then step three is entering the desired state. Enter a state of calmness. And as you're doing this, it's like you're a magnet and step two is you're plugging yourself into them, connecting with them, and step three is, now that you've connected with them, you're lifting yourself up, you're lifting yourself up into a more positive state of mind and you're taking them with you.

And obviously you're talking as you're doing this and you're using stories and you're using language patterns, but often you don't even need to be.

I remember once I was having dinner with a friend of mine and when I greeted him, he seemed really anxious, he was upset about a work problem if I recall. And he was in a pretty sort of frustrated, grumpy state of mind. He was still polite but he wasn't going very well. I, on the other hand, was in a really positive, bouncy, happy state of mind. So, there's an incongruence there, isn't it? One party's really positive and happy; the other party is really negative. There's going to be no rapport there.

So, I just temporarily, just for twenty seconds, dropped myself down into a sort of anxious, frustrated state of mind to match his state. When we were both in that state of mind for just twenty seconds or so and we were right there on that level, I brought myself back into that positive calm state of mind and this time, I brought him with me.

It's not some weird sort of psychic "woo woo" thing, it's just psychological. Remember the mirror neurons concept. People match the emotional states of those they're in rapport with.

However, in order to be in rapport with somebody, it helps if you're in a similar emotional state to them. By dropping yourself down into their emotional state, you can communicate with them eye to eye, on the same wavelength. When you move yourself back up, into a more positive state of mind, you take them with you. As your body language changes, so does their body language change.

It's very, very simple stuff and it's extremely, extremely powerful.

You'll recall the empathy lesson that I taught you a while ago, the "it's not mind reading" lesson, that will give you some really powerful strategies for identifying the state of mind somebody happens to be in.

ABOUT THE AUTHOR

Naresh Kumar is an Author, Mind Coach and Master Trainer of Neuro-Linguistic Programming. He is also an expert in Life Coaching and EFT (Emotional Freedom Techniques). Naresh is passionate about Rapid Change Work. He believes that time is the most precious asset that we have. He uses Rapid Therapy and Rapid Coaching to help his clients in 1:1 and group sessions. He is the founder of NLPMinds (**nlpminds.com**), and has been conducting NLP, Hypnosis and EFT Workshops in India for past half decade. He can be reached at **success@nlpminds.com**.

For more information please visit:

- **http://nlpminds.com**
- **http://nareshkumar.net**